# Preparing for

# SITE – BASED

# RESEARCH

## A RESEARCH PROJECT GUIDE
## FOR GRADUATE STUDIES

**Jim Parsons**
**Laura Servage**

Illustrations by Jocelyn Dimm

# Preparing for
# SITE – BASED
# RESEARCH

## A RESEARCH PROJECT GUIDE
## FOR GRADUATE STUDIES

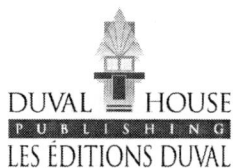

DUVAL HOUSE
PUBLISHING
LES ÉDITIONS DUVAL

5 4 3 2 1
Printed and bound in Canada

Duval House Publishing / Les Éditions Duval, Inc.
18228-102 Avenue
Edmonton, Alberta CANADA T5S 1S7
Phone: 1-800-267-6187
Fax: (780) 482-7213
Web site: www.duvalhouse.com

Authors
Jim Parsons, Laura Servage
Illustrator
Jocelyn Dimm

We acknowledge the financial suppoort of the Government of Canada through the Book Publishing Industry Development Program (BPIDP) for our publishing activities.

Canadä

*In action research you are always venturing into the unknown...*
*sometimes you just gotta go for it.*

# Contents

# *Acknowledgements*

MUCH OF THE INFORMATION on focus groups provided in Chapter 7 is adapted from a collaborative effort by the following graduate students: Sharon Babcock, Ron Duffell, David Huddock, Stuart Hutton, Leah Lawrason, Brigitte McKenzie, Ruth Robertson, Libby Rush, Jennifer Selman, Bev Sieker, and Noreen Taylor.

Material for the section "Conducting Interviews" in Chapter 7 was contributed by graduate students Eva Boyd, Carol Brown, Morgan Fisher, Al Heon, Jody Rebek, Amy Tucker, and Kate Wootton (second residency, 2003).

Special thanks to Jocelyn Dimm for her lively cartoon renditions of key ideas from the book, and to Stacey Ward for her assistance with research.

# *Preface*

**MAKING A DIFFERENCE THROUGH RESEARCH**

**NOT TOO LONG AGO** graduate students attended their programs full time and spent most of their hours on traditional university campuses. Over the past twenty years, however, the profile of graduate students has changed considerably. More and more, we see adult students pursuing higher education because their needs or interests at work put them to it. Graduate studies help students to develop the tools and critical thinking skills they need to solve increasingly complex problems in their fields.

## Who are you as a graduate student?

Below are four loosely accurate descriptions of learners we have worked with. As you read them, allow yourself to understand the backgrounds and desires within these descriptions of learners. Can you see yourself anywhere in these descriptions?

**Building morale and teamwork.** Joanna has worked as a nursing administrator for about ten years. Specifically, her job is to run the emergency ward of a large urban hospital. She has an undergraduate degree in nursing, though it was taken about twenty years ago. She is concerned about the dropping morale of the hospital, especially within her own unit. She recalls that doctors and nurses worked together well as a team; however, she laments that those times seem tied to some mythical point in the past. In her experience, that spirit of teamwork no longer exists. This is sad, she feels, because things used to work so much better.

There was better patient care, more commitment with the medical staff, even—if you can believe it—better healing. Her interest is to see if such teams can become a reality once again. Is it feasible? Is there a will to do it? Does anyone else really care or even see this as an issue?

**An innovative idea.** Ed is a city manager for a mid-sized northern Ontario city. He got to where he is through political savvy and hard work. He has no undergraduate degree. But he is street-smart and a big-picture thinker. Plus he gets things done, and he has united a close-knit group of city workers who are fiercely loyal and committed to the best interests of the city. As one of his political and economic agendas, he is interested in conducting a feasibility study to see whether the school boards—both Catholic and public—and the city can work together to design and build a multifaceted building that would share such things as equipment and secretarial/administrative staff. Is there an interest in such a novel idea? How would it work? Has anyone else anywhere thought of this? And finally, how much real money might it save the taxpayers?

**Sharing a love of nature.** Clyde may not be a teacher by trade, but he is in spirit. He grew up, so his mother said, in the woods and, according to her, would have gathered moss himself except that he never stood still long enough. His education has two aspects: informally, on his own, he has read everything about forestry, and formally, he finished high school, though barely. It just didn't interest him. But he knows every brook and stream, every tree and animal in the forest. Nature is his abiding love, and he wants to share that love with others. He also is concerned about the environment and being a good steward of the earth. He wants to build a curriculum of the woods and to teach others to share his devotion for nature and all that nature contains. He believes he can write a book that would be used during tours he would give. He believes that other people would also be drawn to nature, and he wants them to experience it both first- and second-hand. Right now, without doing any homework, he thinks that people would be interested in a one-week or two-week tour or trek where they could really experience the wonders of nature. He also believes that he can create enough revenue from such an enterprise that he can live from his love. He wants to know the answer to this question: is his idea possible?

**Seeking the dreamer in each of us.** Angelica remembers the story her father told about meeting her junior high language arts teacher. When the father was summoned to the school to hear that his daughter had great ability but tended to dream a lot, his response was to tell the language arts teacher to encourage Angelica to do more of it. This was not exactly the answer the teacher was expecting! And Angelica has since spent time dreaming. She feels more settled on the inside (well, usually) than she seems to others on the outside. She has an undergrad degree in English literature from an American university—she met someone in a Laundromat who invited her to California, she went, and four years later she graduated. She would have a master's degree if all the courses she'd ever taken could be added together; she'd begun further studies about five times over, yet something always called her to quit.

She writes poetry and works with street people in a large Canadian city. She is concerned about how heartless society seems to be, and she wants to inject heart into organizations so that people can realize their dreams. She is a self-confessed "poetry-writing wing nut," but knows she has a gift for writing and encouraging. She wants to write a book entitled *Heart in Work*, but she has never really tried to focus her efforts into that area. Could this, she wonders, be a goal for her graduate work?

---

The students we describe here are the closest we can come to representing anything "typical." But the truth—and the excitement—of graduate work is that it brings diverse people together in a space of intense intellectual activity. Often it is also a time of intense personal growth and soul searching. Graduate students—especially those in interdisciplinary programs—are an eclectic bunch with a great deal to share and much to learn from one another.

However, our experience is that many of you may wonder how much you really have to offer. One thing many students do have in common is a case of impostor syndrome. As we understand it, this means that students worry that they might soon be found out—that they don't actually belong in a graduate-level program and that some dark night there will be a knock on their door and they will be asked to leave, immediately. This is especially the case for mature students—working professionals who have been away from formal studies for a number of years.

## The Rewards and Challenges of Graduate Work

We believe that you are on the cusp of turning and churning your many thoughts about your area of study into a workable vision and plan for conducting research. Research, many tell us, rings like the Spectre of Christmas Yet To Come. This, truly, is facing the unknown. Even if you know what you want to do, there are lingering questions about *how* to do it. Then there is the writing-it-up part. For those of you who have not lived in the world of words, this can look like a test of your abilities. *Preparing for Site-Based Research* is the collection of ideas and processes that have worked with graduate students like you. It contains step-by-step procedures that outline, from start to finish, the undertaking before you—your own research project. We hope this book helps you.

First, we offer advice. Take solace in the fact that many people, similar in background and abilities, have completed the task of graduate work before you. In fact, you would be wise to go on a little field trip to look at the fruit of their labours. Read some theses or final projects created by other graduate students who worked in an area similar to yours. Second, we give you this promise: if you do your part, like those who have gone before you, you will soon be finished. You will then know the secret handshake...but of course, we can't tell you that right now. Later, friends.

## How to Use This Book

Over the course of your program, you will be designing, conducting, and reporting a site-based investigation. You will be doing research. Many of you believe that this research is new to you, and that can be frightening. But in a way you have been preparing for this research all your lives. Research is less rocket science than it is carefully planned and rigorously attended activity. That means that if you have a good project (one worth doing) and you do it well (with care and consideration), you will be able to complete work that "contributes to the literature" (the defining feature of valuable research) and that you will be proud of. No one talks much about the pride of a job well done, but don't underestimate the motivational aspect of prideful work.

One of my standard pieces of advice to new researchers is not to get goofy. Don't run around in a panic, wasting energy gratuitously. You need your energy and calmness of thought. It is one thing to enjoy a hike through the woods; it is quite another to be lost and wandering around in that setting. My wife Tara and I recently came back from hiking in New Zealand. Those of you who have hiked New Zealand's South Island know how well constructed the hiking trails are and how beautiful the scenery is. Some days, we would set out on a hike as long as 30 kilometres. It was hard work, and we (okay, me) were tired when we finished the hike, but the satisfaction and the landscapes were breathtaking. We knew where we were going, because the trails were well laid out. As a result, we could enjoy the hike. And for someone as old as I am, to describe to others the success of walking almost 30 kilometres in a day is exhilarating. Now Tara and I show others our photos, and we enjoy the hike over and over.

Think of this manual as your guided hiking trail, and think of completing your project as a hike along this trail. It will sometimes be tiring, and you should know that up front. Perhaps at some point you will even feel like turning around. But if you know that you are not lost and that eventually you will arrive at the end of the trail, you will be able to look around and truly enjoy the vistas.

We wrote *Preparing for Site-Based Research* to offer you a brief, clear, and detailed look at how to complete your own self-directed site-based research. It provides a framework that will help you complete your own personal written report. The result will be dual: you will have contributed to the literature, and you will have engaged in professional growth.

May your journey be rewarding and meaningful.

JIM PARSONS

# ONE

# *Research*
## IN EDUCATION

*Everybody does research.*

**WE BEGIN AT THE BEGINNING WITH A VERY SIMPLE FACT:** we do research to learn about something that we believe is important or of interest to us. In its basic form, you've probably already filled your life with research activities but haven't named those activities "research." Perhaps you've read books on parenting to learn more about how to raise your kids. Or, you may have visited several dealerships, asked lots of questions, and comparison shopped before buying a new car. Maybe you've been in charge of organizing a Christmas party and have asked around your workplace to get some feel for what people would like to do. In other words, you have consciously set out to gather information for a specific purpose.

## What It Means to Do Research

All research, from highly structured formal laboratory experiments right down to even these simple and informal examples, has these two characteristics in common: (1) there is a conscientious process at work that you (2) undertake for a specific purpose.

Research is *conscientious* in that you are consciously aware that you are in a process of gathering information. This conscious process means that you've probably thought about the best ways to find out what you need to know and that you are paying careful attention to the information as it comes in. Probably, you are organizing it—at least in your head.

You may even have done very "researchy" things like *sampling* your population. For example, to plan your staff Christmas party you may have decided that you didn't need to ask absolutely everyone to get a good feel for what people would like. Using your own discretion, you chose certain people to talk to. Then you asked them a question or questions, and you listened to what they had to say. You did this "research" because their feedback was of direct relevance to something you wanted to accomplish: namely, to hold a Christmas party that everyone would enjoy.

This objective leads us to the second characteristic of research: it is *purposeful.* You don't invest your time, energy, and care into gathering information unless you have some reason to do it. In each of the examples above, the research process had a goal: to become a better parent, to buy a new car, or to throw a good party. In this sense, academic or organizational research is exactly the same. It may employ systems that seem much more complex or may take on much broader or more esoteric objectives: to find out why a consumer product is not selling, to improve student math marks, to help recent immigrants overcome employment barriers, to find a cure for Parkinson's disease. Still, at its most fundamental level, all research is the same—you want to know something, and you work to find it out.

Further, the loftiness or commonness of the research objective has little bearing on how we measure the success of a research project. We do not distinguish parent satisfaction surveys at a local daycare as any more or less "good" than, say, a study of physically abusive childhoods among habitual criminals, experiments in DNA sequencing, or a focus group held among an organization's board of directors. Rather, success is measured by the answer to one simple question: did the research meet its stated objectives with accuracy and integrity?

## Research Objectives

*Is it also important to question is it worth asking?*

As you can probably see by now, we believe a research project can have virtually any objective. But it always *has* an objective! There are many approaches to classifying the types of objectives that guide research. To make these distinctions, we can ask a couple of basic questions.

1. Is the research being conducted simply for the sake of gaining knowledge, or are its results intended to have some practical purpose?
2. How broadly or narrowly can the results be applied?

One way of answering these questions is to sort research activities into two very broad categories: basic research and applied research (OECD 1994).

**Basic research** is undertaken simply for the sake of furthering knowledge. Because it is done for its own sake, it is not often seen outside of academic settings—although if you've ever picked up a book to learn about something "just because you're curious," you could say that you are embracing the spirit of basic research! In its formal sense, basic (or theoretical) research often involves proposing, testing, and developing theories. That is, its purpose is to provide principles that advance knowledge in a certain area of study. Theoretical researchers formulate and test models they believe may apply broadly to their disciplines.

For example, currently much educational research is being done on the human brain: how does it work? What can this understanding tell us about learning (and teaching)? Some brain researchers use an *information-processing model* of the human brain to compare its functions to those of a computer. This theoretical analogy becomes a framework for other researchers to build their ideas upon. Over time, this particular theory has been used as a way of thinking about practical problems in applied research studies. Because it has been a useful model in many and varied circumstances, it has come to be accepted as a credible theory. This is actually the goal of most basic research: to come up with ideas, models, or paradigms that with time and testing come to be accepted as general truths, or perhaps more accurately, as generally valid ways of seeing the world. Simply put, the major objective of basic research is to have its findings apply *as widely and universally as possible.*

However, while theories generated by basic research provide us with helpful ways of framing problems and tasks, they do little beyond this "thinking" stage. For example, if we want to learn about how memory develops in young children, it is hardly helpful for us to simply announce, "Why, the human brain works like a computer!" and leave it at that!

Rather, we might use an information-processing theory to frame this particular study. We say: if we think of the human brain as being like a computer where information is *processed* in short-term memory and *stored* in long-term memory, what can we learn about the strategies that children use to memorize their multiplication tables? In other words, we *apply* the theory to a problem, issue, or phenomenon that we encounter in the real world. This is where we get the notion of applied research.

Unlike basic research, **applied research** does not have abstract, generalizable theories as its goal. Applied research problems have a context. For instance, an applied research project in health care might study the effectiveness of home care follow-ups among the elderly after hospitalization. A study in education might identify large numbers of struggling young readers in a school or district and use what it learns to appeal for special program funding. A hospital CEO might hope to create unit meetings that are more efficient and produce better decision-making results.

Of course, if an applied research study proves effective, it may still be somewhat generalized in that what is learned might be applied in other similar contexts. It may be more helpful, then, to think of generalizability on a continuum (Patton 2002). Applied research, then, means that we learn about, test, and evaluate something we would like to use or apply (hence the name) in a real-world setting. Most research conducted in organizational settings is concerned with the most practical aspects of quality learning and working experiences.

**Fig. 1.1. Research applicability continuum.**

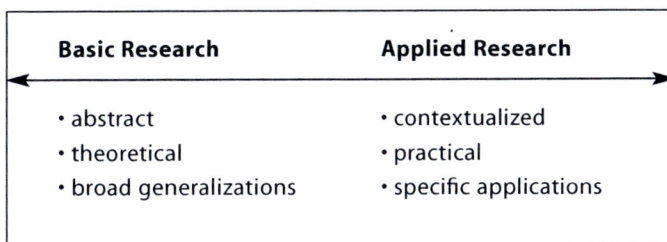

| **Basic Research** | **Applied Research** |
| --- | --- |
| • abstract | • contextualized |
| • theoretical | • practical |
| • broad generalizations | • specific applications |

The research project you will complete falls into the category of applied research. Namely, you will be studying something that you encounter in the real world of your own organization. The purpose of your study is to identify and propose solutions to very specific dilemmas that are uniquely encountered in your own organization's context. In this sense, your research will fall towards the far end of the continuum for specificity. This kind of research—often undertaken by practitioners or workers right within the organization—is a variation of a special category of applied research called action research. We will explore the specific characteristics of **action research** and how it informs your site-based research project in Chapter 2.

**Fig. 1.2. Research objectives.**

|  | Type of Findings Generated | Purpose of Research | Example |
|---|---|---|---|
| **Basic Research** | • findings not bound by context<br>• findings meant to be general<br>• hopefully can be widely applied across situations | • to create principles, theories, or frameworks that someone else can apply to other learning and problem-solving situations | • Medical research on cell regeneration in plants and animals. Problem-solvers might then apply this information to create medical procedures to help stop the rapid spread of Parkinson's disease. |
| **Applied Research** | • more specific than basic research<br>• the researcher may generalize somewhat across similar cases | • to understand and explain a particular type of problem or phenomenon | • using basic research about adolescent psychology to plan coaching strategies for a junior high swim team |
| **Action Research** | • has a very specific context<br>• application is problem solving<br>• no impetus to generalize the research to other settings | • to solve specific problems within specific contexts or settings using any variety of basic research and applied research | • "How can workers in a given organization be encouraged to feel a sense of ownership and pride in their work?" |

## Mapping Research Strategies:
## Methods and Methodology

In the previous section, we talked about research objectives and presented some ways to classify and think about what a research project is trying to achieve. Now we need to consider how we go about accomplishing these objectives. This leads us to the next important stage in any research project: its methods and methodology.

The term *research method* simply refers to a carefully laid-out plan for finding out what you want to know. There are many, many ways to develop a plan, and much of this plan is shaped by the nature of the problem or question that has been identified for research. Considerations that might shape the methods used in a research project include (but are certainly not limited to):

**Ethical concern for your research subjects.** One of the most critical aspects of a research plan is ensuring that your work does not cause harm to others. All organizations that conduct research have ethics review boards that examine research methods to ensure research subjects are protected from physical harm, psychological damage, or other negative effects.

**The availability of data.** Research projects may be constricted in some ways by limited availability of data. If one is researching infant behaviour, for instance, it is obvious that the subjects cannot be asked to verbalize their experiences! Studies of the experiences of Holocaust survivors become increasingly restrictive as these individuals dwindle in number, dying of natural causes.

**Time, money, and other resources available for your study.** Most research projects work within a set budget and time period, so the ideal set-up may not always be feasible. If nothing else, this can force you to be creative about research design! One student we know of, for instance, was unable to conduct a focus group, as the participants were scattered all over three provinces and could not travel. Instead, he set up his "focus group" using an online discussion board. The messages from the board were a valuable source of data, and since they were already in written form, they did not have to be transcribed!

**The amount of research that has already been done in the area.** Some research studies—for instance, those in the areas of leadership and organizational behaviour—are easier to structure and conduct because a large body of work and research literature already exists on the topics. Earlier work in a field goes a long way in shaping and structuring a research project. Where this is absent, the researcher may need considerable personal expertise and resources to develop her work.

**How you want to use your findings.** This is among the trickiest of the factors that shape research methodology—mostly because it is so easy to collect data that do not truly answer the questions asked in your research. We'll explain: say, for instance, that you want to study the effectiveness of an adult literacy program. You might gather data on program attrition rates or the reading levels of program graduates. Do these data really answer your question, though? Perhaps attrition rates have to do with factors outside of the program itself—for instance, participants have trouble obtaining transportation to and from the program. Perhaps lower-than-expected reading scores by graduates do not capture whether the program has been truly "effective" in terms of transforming participants' lives.

You can probably already see that choosing methods is not a simple process! This is one of the reasons that research is both challenging and fascinating; the possible number of research designs is as unlimited as the number of research questions you could ask. Each research problem is uniquely shaped by its goals and context, and in turn, each requires a unique approach in its methodology.

## Methods and Methodology

You'll probably encounter the words *methods* and *methodology* a fair bit in your reading. There is some confusion about these terms and they are not interchangeable! **Method**, as you have already seen, refers to the series of steps chosen to find the answer to your question. Methods are subsumed (or acted upon) within the larger question of methodology. Your **methodology** is more like an overall guiding philosophy; it is your explanation of *why* you chose to approach the question as you did.

Writing a clear methodology is important because it reveals something about those fundamental beliefs that you, as a researcher, hold about the nature of the problem you are investigating. To fully understand your research, your readers need to understand the perspective or worldview you bring to your work. As you will see in our discussion about *researcher bias*, articulating your worldview in your research methodology lends context and understanding to your findings and interpretations.

Briefly, methodology is:

**Philosophical**. When we begin to examine methodologies—our own or those of other researchers—it is almost inevitable that we will venture into questions about what reality is (metaphysics) and how something can truly be "known" (epistemology). You don't need to study philosophy to be philosophical: you may find yourself asking your own particular versions of these questions quite naturally if you are careful and reflective about your research work.

**Normative**. Always inherent in methodology are assumptions both about how the world is organized and about how it *should* be organized. Early positivist perspectives claimed objectivity was key in research. Today, most researchers believe that research cannot be value-free.

**Paradigmatic**. In 1962, philosopher Thomas Kuhn proposed that scientific inquiry is shaped by great, sweeping paradigms or metaphors about how the world works. Collectively, our way(s) of seeing the world can be so entrenched, so taken-for-granted, and so constantly reinforced that it is almost impossible for us to imagine viewing reality any other way.

For your introduction to research, we've considered only two basic paradigms of research: *quantitative* and *qualitative*. These are broad categories, but they capture and represent many of the tensions and issues surrounding reality and how it is represented (remember, philosophy is at the heart of research). These tensions are sorted out and, for the purposes of your own work, at least, temporarily pinned down in your methodology.

## Quantitative Research

The idea of creating a research methodology may appear quite daunting. In our experience, when most people think of research, they seem intimidated by visions of lab technicians poking rats, hieroglyphic-like statistical analyses, and lengthy incomprehensible reports. They believe that academics can do it, but they cannot. The research you will be conducting is nothing like this! In fact, most popular or common notions about what research is come from a **quantitative research** paradigm.

*We use measurements to separate the world into small pieces so we can study them.*

Quantitative research emerges from Western intellectual traditions. Chiefly, it is *empirical*. This means that what we "discover" with this kind of research are experiences through the senses, which can and should be measured. These measurements are used to break the world into small pieces and to study these separate pieces under microscopic rigour. In this sense, quantitative research is *deductive*: a "big idea" or general theory (which is usually stated in a hypothesis) is tested by looking at whether individual facts support it, and the facts are those things that we can perceive with our senses and *count* up in some way.

When we count up these data, we are aggregating them; individual cases or responses are not so important. Instead, the data as a whole are analyzed for any significant patterns—this is where the math and statistical analysis comes in. We might compare two groups, one of which received a treatment and one which is a control group—for instance, when testing the effectiveness of a new drug— or we might try to find a cause that links two phenomena together. Public opinion polls are another obvious example of collecting and analyzing statistics.

Organizing human experiences with statistics can tell us a great deal. For example, statistical analyses have generally found a correlation (a link) between low income and poor health (Chappell 1998). While we may still be left to speculate on why exactly this correlation exists, simply *knowing* it exists can be helpful. A new health clinic setting up in an inner-city neighbourhood might look at statistics like household income to make some predictions about the amount and types of needs and services that might be important to focus on. In another example, the clinic might look at statistics and note that the population in the area is quite young. Based on this information, the clinic decides to develop education programs on prenatal health and prevention of sexual disease.

Gathering such data is a careful process. Quantitative research utilizes specific methods, or recipes, to conduct systematic studies. These are carefully delineated so that others might repeat experiments under the same conditions. When the same conditions produce the same results each time, the phenomenon under inquiry is established as factual or "true." Actually, we state that "the research supports the following hypothesis:...." We use quotations around words like *true* because this is, of course, a simple explanation. Proving some- thing empirically is usually a lengthy and complicated process, and much of what is learned is still regarded with a healthy degree of skepticism.

We reserve our greatest skepticism about "truth" for the most complex and unpredictable of subjects to study—our brother and sister human beings! *Qualitative* research emerged as we recognized that *quantitative* approaches— while generally a comfortable fit for the hard sciences—did not in all cases effectively capture the complexity, diversity, and subtlety of human experience. Much of what we are is maddeningly (or wonderfully) immeasurable and uncountable and therefore unquantifiable—like trying to count love.

*Qualitative research builds complex,
holistic pictures of the world.*

## Qualitative Research

**Qualitative research**, then, comes from a very different paradigm. Generally, it is characterized as an inquiry process with methodologies that explore social or human problems. It is research that tries to describe a phenomenon (quality), not count it (quantity). To complete qualitative research, a researcher must build a complex, holistic picture, analyze words, report detailed views of informants, and usually conduct the study in a natural setting (Creswell 1998).

We can compare quantitative and qualitative research on several fronts. First, you'll recall that quantitative research is generally a *deductive* process—one that proposes a theory and seeks facts to support it. Qualitative research is, by contrast, *inductive* or *emergent*. In other words, the process is stood on its head: the theory—or perhaps more accurately, the interpretation—*emerges* from the data. This is often also referred to as *open-ended inquiry*, because the researcher enters the scene with a "Hmm, I wonder what I'll find out" sort of approach. While a guiding or focusing question or set of questions begins the process, it is common—and quite acceptable—for these questions to mutate in response to what the research finds out along the way. This stands in direct opposition to quantitative research questions, which are carefully constructed and must be answered directly for the study to be considered valid.

We also stated that quantitative research is empirical—a notion that emerges in science that is more Western and industrial/technical in character. Qualitative research also makes considerable use of sensory observations, but it can be more open to the felt or *subjective* experiences that empirical studies actually strive to eliminate or control by being as *objective* as possible. We might say that qualitative research is East to the science of the West, the yin for the yang, with a receptivity to the nuanced, unique characteristics of the given problem or context.

One particular expression of this distinction is in the research *setting*. Quantitative studies carefully control the research setting so that it does not bias findings; in other words, contextual factors are, as much as possible, eliminated or neutralized. Very often, quantitative studies are also quite artificial and may take place in laboratory settings. For qualitative research, however, context is part of what the study is all about; the researcher wants to know how people behave, think, and feel in their own environments (Bogdan and Biklen 1992). Because this research is holistic in character, it focuses on understanding the entire environment within which a research problem "lives" and paints as complete a picture of that context as possible. The setting of the research is *naturalistic*, in that it "takes place in the real world...and the researcher does not attempt to manipulate the phenomenon of interest" (Patton 2002). In fact, we often speak of fieldwork in qualitative inquiry, using the term as it emerged from studies in anthropology and natural sciences (Bogden and Biklin 1992). The researcher is "in the field" when she is observing and/or interacting with her subjects in their own environment.

Because qualitative research is rather context-specific, it is less generalizable than quantitative studies. However, you'll recall that being general is much less of a goal for qualitative researchers. In qualitative approaches, the individual case is more important than aggregating and generalizing data.

*interactions with people on pool deck not considered due to inability to confirm the other person due to distance*

**Fig. 1.3.**

**Characteristics of qualitative research and quantitative research.**

| Quantitative Research | Qualitative Research |
|---|---|
| • measures phenomena | • describes phenomena |
| • deductive | • inductive |
| • studies the world in small, discrete pieces | • studies the world as an organic whole |
| • goal is to generalize findings to the larger world | • findings often apply in specific contexts |
| • the researcher should be objective and unbiased | • the researcher's subjectivity is inevitable, acknowledged, and sometimes even embraced |
| • the setting is controlled and artificial | • the setting is natural |

## *Which to Choose?*

It should be emphasized that both major paradigms—quantitative and qualitative—have a legitimate role to play in research. The choice of one over the other (or in some cases, a decision to use strategies from both) depends on the research question to be answered. Both types of research may study the same research issue—say, the emergence of dot-com companies—with very different kinds of information emerging. Quantitative research might focus upon the financial growth (or losses) of these companies, charting a graph of their profits in response to a particular government decision (like the decision to regulate Napster). Qualitative research might focus upon the *lifeworlds* of the young entrepreneurs who start such companies, wondering about aspects of their family backgrounds that could encourage creativity and challenge or cause a rebellious nature towards traditional rules—anything that would explain how these young people came to think outside the box.

In some cases, we use elements of both quantitative and qualitative methods in our research design. If, for example, we were to gather statistical data on employee satisfaction with a long-term, in-house training program, we might learn that 78 percent of participating staff were satisfied or very satisfied with the program. These are quantitative data, and they are valuable because they tell us that the training program is doing a pretty good job.

What it doesn't tell us is the impact of the program on individual employees. Case studies or focus groups—qualitative methods that allow us to explore subjects in depth—might reveal insights that we would not have gained from statistics; for instance, that one of the reasons the training had been so well received was because Human Resources had been particularly sensitive and helpful throughout the process, or because staff had developed deeper, closer relationships with one another through the training.

It is also worth restating that the differences between quantitative research and qualitative research are not always hard and fast. They are two paradigms, two different approaches to problem solving, but this does not mean that you have to religiously adhere to one or the other (although some people do!). Many researchers (ourselves included) take an eclectic approach to methodology, employing either quantitative and qualitative strategies where most useful. A couple of examples may help here to further clarify what is usually referred to as a *mixed methods* approach.

**Example 1.** *A researcher observing preschoolers in a community play group uses an observation checklist, counting certain behaviours that he observes. For instance, on a given day he may observe and tally x instances of verbal aggression and x instances of physical aggression. Here the researcher is observing in the field and supplementing his counts with jotted observations that he will later turn into rich descriptions of the play group setting. These are "qualitative-ish" characteristics. However, the fact that he is also counting specifically defined behaviours leans more towards a quantitative approach.*

**Example 2.** *Another researcher is trying to evaluate the recreational programming at a senior's lodge. The main source of her data is a survey that asks residents to identify which* *programs they have accessed and to indicate on a scale of one to five how satisfied they were with each program. She also uses documents to review participation rates in the programs over the past five years. The data she is collecting are countable and therefore quantitative. However, she also includes some open-ended questions on her survey so that participants can respond freely with their own thoughts and ideas. While the bulk of her report will be drawn from the numeric data she has gathered, she will use participant comments to give a sense of their experiences with the program.*

In each of the examples above, you can probably see where the quantitative and qualitative research methods can complement and support one another in their findings. We call this complement *triangulation*, whereby approaching the same problem from different angles (or different methods) improves the accuracy and validity of the research findings. We will discuss triangulation and validity in much greater detail in Chapter 6.

**Fig.** 1.4.

**Some basic types of research.** (Adapted from Fraenkel & Wallen 2003.)

## Quantitative (Statistical) Studies

**Experimental**          Use a treatment group and a control group to study the effects of some experimental intervention. For example, we might try two different reading programs with two groups of grade one students and compare the results that each program achieves.

**Correlational**          Correlational studies look for links between two phenomena. An example of a well-known correlation is the link between age and risk-taking behaviour. An important thing to remember about correlations, however, is that they show only a relationship between two variables, not the *cause* of that relationship.

**Causal-Comparative**          Unlike correlation studies, causal-comparative experiments have the objective of determining the *causal direction* of two linked phenomena. What factors, for instance, might determine an adult's level of physical fitness? A study might examine family history, eating habits, or other lifestyle factors. Often, however, establishing cause is chicken-and-egg stuff: quite difficult to do with real certainty!

## Qualitative (Descriptive) Studies

**Case Study**          Also called single-subject research, a case study is a qualitative research method that focuses with great detail on a particular person or group. For instance, a highly effective organization (or an abysmally failing one) might be studied for practical lessons that might be applied to other, similar programs. *Description* is important to case study research.

| | |
|---|---|
| **Ethnographic** | Ethnographic research is similar to case studies in that it is highly focused and descriptive. Its flavour is a little different, though, in that it generally attempts to create rich portraits of everyday life. There is less emphasis on how the research will be used. |
| **Historical** | Historical research uses documents (and perhaps interviews) to study something that has occurred in the past. In organizational settings, such information can provide a valuable context for present-day concerns. For instance, revealing a lengthy history of conservative management and corporate culture might go a long way in explaining why a particular organization is very resistant to change. |

## About Bias: Situating the Researcher

Another important distinction between quantitative and qualitative strategies is the role of the researcher within the research itself. Quantitative research methods are highly structured, because those who practise quantitative research depend upon the careful application of specific methods in an attempt to avoid human bias and therefore human error. The relationship between researcher and subjects is—at least as far as methods are concerned—a non-relationship because the researcher does not want his presence to influence or interfere with the subjects in any way. This is not to say that all quantitative research relationships are these cold, robotic sorts of things. But it is to say that the researcher attempts to be more cautious and structured in her approach, and works hard to not allow any human relationship to compromise the research work.

As an example, say that a researcher wants his subjects to view movie clips containing varying degrees of aggression and violence. After the viewing, the subjects fill out a questionnaire that asks them to agree or disagree with a number of statements. The researcher is trying to determine whether viewing aggressive material increases aggressive behaviour and attitudes. To make sure that subjects are influenced only by what they have watched and not by something he has said, the researcher must make a point of being very consistent in his approach. He will give—usually read—the exact same instructions to each person he studies, perhaps even using a script. Some researchers will not answer questions that research subjects ask, so that one subject will not have additional insight that another does not have.

While avoiding researcher bias in carefully controlled laboratory conditions may seem fairly straightforward, life conspires to get a little murkier when we start collecting data in the field. First, avoiding bias isn't really viewed as a problem in qualitative research. Instead, human biases are acknowledged as perspectives that are important and which must be understood. Within the qualitative paradigm, it is believed that there can be no research without researcher bias. In fact, the bias of the researcher is always present, and it can help the reader of qualitative research better understand how the research was seen and done. For this reason, qualitative researchers often spend a great deal of time attempting to explain their biases at the beginning of any research study. The rationale here is simple: the more you know about the person, the more you can understand the research.

Acknowledging that (1) bias exists, and (2) bias is not such a bad thing, allows the qualitative researcher more latitude in the types of relationships she can form with her participants. Methodologically, it is not wrong to enter the subjective world of the research subject(s); in fact, it is desirable! And, the best way to achieve this understanding is to talk with and spend time with research subjects, often participating in their daily lives in what is called (logically, it seems to us) participatory research.

For some, the element of bias in qualitative research—particularly in its more intimate and participatory forms—simply makes research invalid or unscientific. Researchers may be chastised for imposing their own perspectives on what they study, and it is true that some research is simply so idiosyncratic as to render it goofy. However, acknowledging and working with your biases doesn't mean that you as the researcher give your perspective utterly free rein. The researcher's job, after all, is to represent the situation as fairly and accurately as possible. Responsible researchers do their best to be conscious of personal biases that shape their perceptions and subsequent accounts of their work.

# Conclusion

Many people (ourselves included) believe that the true value of research is determined not by nitpicking about which research approach is superior (although some academics love to do this) but by returning to the original question of whether the study furthers the objectives it sets out to achieve. It is easy to get bogged down in details, enough so that you lose the big picture. Rather than participate in the age-old religious arguments about how many angels can dance on the head of a pin, perhaps we would simply be interested in meeting, interviewing, and learning about a single one of those dancing angels!

As an illustration, we recently heard a high-level civil servant suggest that the educational research being done in the province of Alberta should avoid a research problem called the Hawthorne effect. The Hawthorne effect basically says that we don't want researchers treating subjects as special and having them perform better—that is, learn more—because of the special treatment. From a quantitative research perspective, this is a problem. But think about that statement for a moment. Treating students as special so that they learn more is a cornerstone of excellent teaching! In fact, we pray that we do this and do it well. Why would we want our research to avoid this influence?

The lesson here is that research design should serve the research objectives, not the other way around. In this chapter we've provided some theory to give you a foundation for choosing your own research design, but theory should not be the lone guide or determinant of your inquiry: this amounts to the tail wagging the dog!

As we've emphasized throughout this chapter, your research can draw from *any* theoretical perspectives and combinations of methodology so long as it is conducted ethically, with your commitment to, as best as you can, "tell the truth" about the organizational issue you are studying. The goal? To further knowledge about that organization so that improvements can be made in the lives of the people who live and work there.

# TWO

**ABOUT**

# *Action Research*

*Hmm, I wonder what I'll find out.*

**BECAUSE SITE-BASED RESEARCH EMPLOYS MANY OF THE SAME PRINCIPLES** and methods as action research, it makes sense to explore action research in more detail. Although your project may not necessarily follow all aspects of the action-reflection cycle explained below, it is helpful to understand the process and have a feel for how action research works in practice. We have focused on action research because we believe the principles of action research hold the greatest promise for helping researchers gain the greatest insight and make the most promising changes in their own practice.

## Defining Action Research

Patton (2002) classifies research activities along a continuum with the most theoretical, abstract, and generalizable at one end (what we called "basic research") and the most specific and practical at the other (what we called "applied research"). Action research and its variants—including what we have named site-based research—rest comfortably in the latter category: they are specific and practical; they propose or result in actions that attempt to improve organizations.

Action research is undertaken basically as a way to improve the work of an organization. A secondary impact of action research is the professional growth and learning that takes place as the research is done. One does not simply conduct research; one learns deeply about the topic and situation in which the research is conducted—that is, if the research is done "right." Any staff person in an organization might employ action research when an organizational issue is seen as a problem to solve or an opportunity to explore. It is seldom the case that problems will simply go away, and it is unlikely that less systematic approaches (sort of a spray-and-pray strategy) are sufficient to solve a problem. To make lasting and important changes, you must commit to a process that leads to such change. This is why we value organizational research in the first place.

Thus, action research provides a structure or framework for change. Although there is no hard and fast orthodoxy—no one "right way" to do action research—most action research projects follow a typical action-reflection framework. Here, in all simplicity, it is.

1.  Use reflection and observation to identify aspects of the organization that might be improved upon.
2.  State and consider a research question or problem.
3.  Employ a systematic methodology to gather data about the research problem.
4.  Analyze and report the data. (At all stages, evaluate the work to make certain it is done as well as conceivably possible.)

5. Consider and report the research findings (solutions or ideas for improvement) to the audience who cares most.
6. Implement and evaluate recommended changes.
7. Use evaluations and further reflections to inform future changes and problem-solving scenarios.

Whether these steps are undertaken by an individual teacher examining problems or phenomena in her classroom or by the staff of a particular department or even by an entire institution, the process is always one of systematic reflection and then systematic research "action." But because one guess is seldom enough—you simply cannot know the lay of the land until you walk it— a researcher or research team will continually revisit the research project over its duration, considering work to date, seeking feedback from colleagues, and evaluating outcomes according to the research objectives.

*Researchers build upon each other's ideas.*

Such systematic evaluation may even prompt new research questions, leading to more changes. All this makes better sense if those completing the research remember that their work should be made public and that it should become part of a lasting conversation about improvement for those who live within the organization. Action research is best done by an in-house team.

This research process may take place over several days or several years, but it always involves *praxis*—literally, a concept taken from the Greek meaning "informed, rational, or intentional"—practices. Any action research project should be undertaken in a cyclical fashion in which action is reflected upon and that reflection then informs new actions. Over time, praxis becomes embedded in the culture of an organization, with the ultimate objective being more than specific resolutions to specific problems. Rather, ideally, the outcome is the creation of an entire working climate that is collaborative, creative, flexible, and able to facilitate change in ways that are both organizationally efficient and healthy for individual staff members. If there ever were such a thing as a "learning community," it would be one that engaged in real action research.

As you can probably see, we define action research more as a general philosophy than a specific system. This makes action research more flexible than traditional conceptions of qualitative and quantitative research. Its objectives are different. Its success is not measured in terms of academic rigour or widespread applicability, but in the degree to which it results in organizational improvement. Perhaps good action research can be replicated in another situation, but then, perhaps not. Similarly, although your own site-based research must adhere to the academic requirements of your program, it will be more valuable in the longer term for the potential insights and improvements it offers for your organization.

## Characteristics of Action Research

Action research often has several other features that distinguish it from more traditional forms of research.

**Action research is collaborative.** Earlier we suggested that in quantitative research the researcher is distant from the subjects; his involvement and interaction with subjects is considered a researcher bias, and the attempt is made to eliminate any and all biases. In traditional qualitative research, the researcher usually holds the primary responsibility for interpreting and reporting the meaning of findings. That is, the researcher has a really big role in the research. Participants may be peripherally involved and may be asked to confirm that the study results are accurate portrayals of their situation, but perspectives and understandings are ultimately funnelled through and shaped by the researcher.

In contrast, action research usually encourages participants and researchers to work closely *together* to analyze concrete cases within their own immediate areas of concern and to collaboratively determine their causes, meanings, and solutions. In this special way, action research actually depends upon widespread and egalitarian *participation*. Instead of "researcher" and "research subject(s)," we think of all those involved in the process as *stakeholders*, each having a vested interest in the study at hand, each holding an important perspective, and each responsible to work in considered ways. An action researcher may be conducting the study, but he is far from working alone. As a result, to conduct an action research project well, a researcher should seek and attempt to understand the insights of those others who make up the organizational community.

The underlying assumption fuelling action research is that workers in organizations have been a long-neglected source of expertise. A receptionist may have worked in an office for longer than any of her superiors and over the years watched the culture of her organization change under different managers. A teacher's assistant may be the one more attentive to morale problems in a school than any other member on staff. An accounts receivable clerk may bring an entirely different perspective to client relations than the sales staff. Nurses may witness inefficiencies in their emergency ward that never reach the ears of administrative staff. In action research, a major objective is to bring this hidden expertise into the open by inviting those who encounter the problem or issue in their daily working lives to participate actively in the research process. For this reason, action research is often also referred to as *participatory action research*.

The best action research always involves partnerships—workers within an organization who form a research team. This team may hopefully also include more traditional researchers—those generally found in universities, professional organizations, independent consulting firms, or government agencies. When such a relationship works, it promises that an organization's insiders and outsiders can take advantage of the different insights, expertise, and perspectives each partner brings to the situation.

Collaboration may take place at any or all stages of the research process. Today, those who participate in action research typically follow a collaborative research process that includes:

- staff (practitioner) development of research questions with a discussion of potential personal or institutional expectations and outcomes
- participation in the research process by both workers and researchers
- ongoing dialogue to focus and refocus the research itself and the impact and meanings of the findings
- ongoing negotiations about the conditions or requirements necessary for successful research collaboration.

Because collaboration is a significant and continuous aspect of the work, regular communication among stakeholders is important.

**Action research is empowering.** The participatory nature of action research is based on the philosophical understanding that all research is implicitly political in nature. In a situation where we really want to hear from those who have the greatest interest, it is simply not good enough that the responsibility for research be handed over to "research experts." It is not that such experts are *bad*; it is just that—try as hard as they might to not be—they are, like all humans, biased. It is the sort of bias that implicitly believes (and acts from the belief) that everyone would naturally be interested in the same things you are. Therefore, we shape the research problem we see through our own interests, which may or not be the interests of those who live and work within the situation being studied.

The history of "pure" research is fraught with examples of research experts substituting personal interests, needs, and insights for the needs of those researched. The result may be that though their research might have been done correctly and honestly, its findings amount to very little in terms of addressing real on-the-job needs. Outsiders simply don't and can't know enough.

A common criticism of academic research—especially relating to the social sciences and education—is that "expert" findings have little bearing or applicability to real-world situations. There are still—and you may have met them— university researchers who believe in the value of only those academic publications listed in *esoteric*, scientific databases. (We use the word esoteric here to mean "uncommon" or "obscure.") Not that these journals are poor; it is simply that they are not always accessible to practitioners in the field. Such academic research is typically written *by* and *for* academics, not for wider audiences. In education, for instance, we've met few teachers who seek out hard-core academic studies to inform their daily work. We believe that, if research is to work, it must be shared more openly with a wider audience.

Simply put, action research is not the same sort of research found in many traditional academic journals. It works from the convictions that (1) research should be accessible to everyone; (2) everyone should be given the opportunity to do research; and (3) the greater the researcher's distance from the research site, the less likely it is that the interests of that researcher match the interests of those within that site.

Often in the past, expert recommendations have been imposed from the top down, with no regard, or at least with little sensitivity, to knowledge, needs, or problems as experienced by those who work on the organization's front lines. We believe that educational researchers should work to change this history. Therefore, action research (and your own site-based research) builds knowledge and directs change from the bottom up by utilizing the expertise of those who live and work with organizational problems and care most about finding their solutions: the workers and practitioners who often possess tacit, informal, and on-the-job knowledge. By inviting workers to be full participants in the site-based research process, they become *stakeholders* in the organization's change rather than reluctant experimental subjects of "the next big thing" that managers or administrators want to try out.

The fundamental belief is that such a research approach also helps stakeholders gain feelings of personal efficacy and community in workplaces. We all know that an initiative is more likely to succeed when everyone buys in. We also know that where we've had a hand in creating that initiative, we are more likely to support it. We are interested in doing and understanding research because we care about its impact and possibilities. We believe research can empower us to make positive changes in our situation and the people who live there.

Of course, empowerment has gotten a bad rap in many organizations where the term has been flung about without any adherence to the spirit of its intent. Some years ago, Laura worked in an organization that, after an intensive weekend workshop, declared itself empowered. At a routine staff meeting, the department director informed staff that empowerment was now a part of the way they did their jobs, whether they liked it or not. Apparently, he missed the irony of ordering people to feel empowered. Staff rolled their eyes and grumbled that the workshop had been a waste of time; nothing had changed.

Nothing changed because management had failed to take the leap and trust its own staff to initiate and carry out positive changes; instead, management maintained an iron grip on the pettiest of office procedures. Real empowerment gives workers a sense of control over their day-to-day lives in their organizations and a sense of ownership over both problems and solutions. It is not a "thing" that is handed over in a weekend workshop or that magically leaps off the pages of a book—no matter what a given consultant might tell you!

There is, within action research, a research stream called **emancipatory research**. Emancipatory research carries research goals a bit further: researchers work to identify inequities embedded in social institutions, interactions, and ideologies. Their goal is to develop a moral understanding based on ethical caring and social justice. Empowerment of research participants may move beyond the research *process* to be stated as a deliberate intended *outcome* of the project. Action research, as expressed by emancipatory research, can be used as a basis for institutional reform, wherein workers become political actors and the effects of their political work may be quantitatively and qualitatively measured over time.

Action researchers may also do self-study inquiries into their own lives that consider their personal experiences and build theories that derive from these experiences. Action research provides a conceptual base and employs methods that can be used to consider social, cultural, and historical practices, to critique existing and emerging organizational theories and practices, and to study actions in social institutions within organizations. The bottom line for action research is that it encourages people within the situation of the research to participate in discussions about the conditions that facilitate or inhibit their development within their own organization.

**Action research is practical.** Here's an example of a practical action research project. Heather had recently assumed editorial responsibilities for her school district's monthly newsletter. The district administrators felt that a newsletter would be an important communication tool for their four hundred plus teachers and employees, and wanted it both to provide important informa- tion and to build positive feelings among staff. Unfortunately for this new editor, the newsletter she was handed hadn't to date achieved either objective. Both print and email versions of the newsletter quickly found their way into the circular file. Feedback suggested that the newsletter was irrelevant and dull. Heather wondered what sorts of changes needed to be made to the newsletter to get the district's staff to read and enjoy it.

Heather's dilemma is typical of the types of problems we face in our working lives. We aren't (at least, most of us aren't) looking to discover the meaning of life when we go to work; mostly we strive to do our jobs well and to enjoy good relationships with others as we do so. Our work objectives are generally concrete and practical; so, too, are the types of barriers that prevent us from achieving them.

In its principles, action research recognizes our need to live and work more effectively, and as such, it is invested with a degree of pragmatism. Highly esoteric or theoretical work is neither required nor desired in an action research project; what matters is whether the research leads to effective solutions. Theory may be fine in theory, but in action research theory is useful only if it can be applied to a specific issue within the organization. Essentially, as we noted earlier, action research is not a method of its own. It borrows from the structure, methodology, and ethical considerations of a wide variety of new and traditional research methods, but uses these flexibly to suit the needs of the situation.

One consequence of this flexibility is that action research methodologies may be quite eclectic, employing any and many traditional research data-collection techniques. These include questionnaires, interviews, observations, focus groups, and the examination of documents. Whatever research methods are needed to gain the kinds of insights necessary to improve practice within the organization are considered appropriate.

Reporting methods can be equally eclectic. Whereas traditional research is usually communicated in formal written reports (although this is changing), action research may be reported in any way that best communicates its findings to stakeholders. Reports, videos, stories, presentations, posters, and conferences may be used. The focus is on practicality, which very often is determined by the unique culture of the organization.

**Action research is situated.** Often, reporting will be shaped by the organization's existing culture. For example, academic institutions typically communicate in written form. However, just because a traditional written form is standard within an academic institution does not mean those who complete their research as graduate students must report their work only in writing. One of the first lessons a good communicator learns is to understand the needs of the audience he or she hopes to communicate with. It follows that researchers who are committed to their tasks will seek the most appropriate reporting forms for the audiences with whom they are communicating.

Some institutions or audiences—like government offices and hospitals—may be more comfortable with a conservative style that uses statistical data and formal third-person language. Police officers want "just the facts, ma'am." Others—for example, parents of preschoolers—might appreciate less formal reporting methods that use more practical language than "educationaleze."

Every organization is unique and operates in a unique context. Perhaps it seems silly to make such an obvious statement, but too often we have seen well-intentioned programs, action plans, and reforms implemented in organizations with no consideration for the characteristics that make those organizations what they are. The result is often confusion and ineffectiveness; at worst it simply creates resentment on the part of the subjects (or victims?) of the treatment du jour.

In his book *The Seven Habits of Highly Effective People*, Stephen Covey suggests that we "seek first to understand" (1989, p. 235). Perhaps he was reworking that old maxim that we have two ears and one mouth in order that we should listen twice as much as we speak. Covey's work typically refers to relationships with other people, but he might equally have addressed our organizational environments. The point is, we must seek to understand our surroundings before we go madly off in all directions recommending changes.

Thus when we say that action research is *situated*, we mean that it begins with attention to the context within which the problem is occurring. Because context is so important to problem solving in action research, it is usually inappropriate to generalize findings beyond the organization in which an action research project is conducted. In other words, the findings of one action research study would not necessarily be applicable in another organizational setting. For this reason, action research differs from a more general sense of applied research—where it is expected that the findings can indeed apply more widely.

This is not to say, however, that it is fruitless to read and understand other action research projects. Research sites differ, but they also share similarities. Thus, it is likely that successful action research projects in one site can inform the solutions to problems or issues in another site. It is a fruitful activity to discuss and learn from each other as action researchers.

Because action research is site-specific, it usually is created in a way unique to the organization in which it is to be undertaken. As a result, a researcher is not tied to a strict and specific research methodology. You'll recall that we mentioned that action research is typically classified as qualitative research; however, it is truer that an action research project is a plan for research that needn't subscribe to a certain paradigm. Remember, an action research approach is pragmatic and eclectic. Because this is so, an action researcher may employ any variety of research methodologies and approaches—whatever is appropriate to complete the research and work towards a solution for the problem in question. As we mentioned before, action research is more a philosophy or an attitude than a certain set of research steps.

**Fig. 2.1. Strengths of action research.** (Schmuck 1997.)

| Action research is a valuable form of inquiry because it is: | |
|---|---|
| **Practical** | Concrete, practical improvements are the objective. |
| **Participatory** | Anyone affected by the problem can participate meaningfully. |
| **Empowering** | All participants can contribute, and all can benefit from the process. |
| **Interpretive** | Meaning is constructed using participants' situational realities. |
| **Tentative** | There are not always right answers; rather, possible solutions are negotiated from multiple viewpoints. |
| **Critical** | Participants look critically at problems and act self-critically. |

## What does an action research project look like?

*An action research project undertaken by an Alberta school division demonstrates the genesis and conduct of this type of project and the ongoing, collaborative nature of action research.*

Prior to December 2002, in the Peace River area of Alberta, the Holy Family School Division became concerned that their students were eating poorly. They also believed that the schools themselves exacerbated the problems by offering a steady diet of junk food via canteens and vending machines. Through reading a number of reports on the topic, the school division had also become further convinced that there were huge correlations between healthy minds and healthy bodies. How could their young people learn if the "fuel" they placed in their bodies' tanks was less than energizing?

Because they had a sense of the problem but were unsure of what to do, they contacted the Faculty of Education at the University of Alberta. Two faculty members travelled to Peace River and met with people from the Holy Family School Division to discuss their needs and the possibilities for a project to address those needs. As this group met and talked, it decided that the people with the most vested interests in the project were, in fact, the children. Rather than foist another rule upon students, why not discuss the issue, present the findings and data, and see what emerged? The promise was that a huge educational opportunity existed and that, perhaps, the young students themselves might take ownership of the issue. Otherwise, the project might devolve into just another grownup colonizing activity in the lives of school kids.

Representative upper elementary and junior high students from schools across the Peace Country were invited for a large focus group at the school board office in Peace River. More than thirty young people from a variety of schools attended. There, facilitated by the two University of Alberta Faculty of Education members, the young people read, listened to the problem seen by the schools, considered, and talked through the issues as they saw it. At the end of the day's session, they came up with an action plan that included (1) educating other young people about "Healthy Minds, Healthy Bodies," and (2) working with the school administration to change some of the food practices within the district.

The next step was for these young people to meet and discuss the issues, both financial and practical, for the schools. These meetings happened in late spring 2003. From these meetings, a number of negotiated changes were implemented.

Currently, these changes are in place and being monitored. The commitment of the school district and the students is to regularly evaluate the successes or failures of the plan and to meet to discuss and plan changes that will, in the long run, create more healthy minds and healthy bodies. Although the results of these changes are not final, the goals have not changed. Not only are students and school district staff alike learning more about health and nutrition, they are also learning more about participatory democracy and decision making. For both, the quest for the ideal is being negotiated in the realm of the practical. The process is a situated-in-reality, recursive, and ongoing problem-solving venture—a classic example of action research within an organization.

This action research story nicely exemplifies the strengths of action research. In the reading, did you find aspects that were *participatory, practical, empowering, interpretive, tentative* and *critical?*

## *Characteristics of Action Research: A Summary*

1.  Action research is more a frame of mind than a specific research methodology. It is a democratic, problem-solving approach researchers take towards their own activities and the areas of concern others bring to them. Action research is a process for encouraging positive change (Bogdan and Biklen 1992). This process-oriented approach brings together participants and researchers from a wide variety of disciplines such as academia, law, sports, science, the arts, politics, insurance, energy, labour, hospitality, media, police, public service, and entrepreneurial areas (Duggan and Reid 1999).

2. Action research is a process of inquiry that enables professionals to identify job-related problems, to determine and comprehend the variety of organizational dynamics, and to seek negotiated strategies aimed at improvement.

3. The action research process can result in: (a) professional development, (b) a process of change, (c) enhanced personal awareness, (d) improved practice, and (e) new learning (Alberta Teachers Association 2000).

4. Action research is collaborative in nature and is one form of practitioner research.

5. Action research involves individuals working in their own areas of specialization.

6. Action research can provide researchers with the opportunity to examine a practical problem within a workplace.

**Fig.** 2.2. **Values in action research.** (Stringer 1999.)

**Action research is a worthwhile form of inquiry because it is:**

- **democratic**, enables participation by all people

- **equitable**, acknowledges all people's worth

- **liberating**, provides alternatives to oppressive conditions

- **life-enhancing**, enables the expression of people's human potential

# Can Anyone Do Action Research?

Because action research encourages the participation of laypersons who often lack an academic background in research, traditionally oriented researchers have at times declared that action research is not "real" research. (You may even be wondering if your own project is "real" research—especially if you are new to graduate work.) The challenge then deserves some attention, for a number of reasons.

*We are not doing classic academic research*

First, we need to remember that, in many ways, we are comparing apples to oranges. Classic academic research is fairly formal and emerges from a long tradition of carefully constructed theories and methodologies. Researchers are bound by these traditions and must adhere to them. In other words, they must follow the rules (or steps) of their specific research methodology. If they do not, their work will lack merit and credibility, both within and beyond the academic community.

The premise of action research is quite different. As action (or site-based) researchers, we measure merit simply by judging whether the research and resulting recommendations for change create improvements in the organization. Are working conditions better? Has morale or communication improved? Do the changes enhance efficiency? Are clients or customers more satisfied? Within the bounds of what is decent, ethical, and fair, in action research the ends justify the means. More specifically, technical weaknesses in methodology can be forgiven when the outcomes are clearly beneficial. "Real" action research is that which generates positive change.

That said, we should offer a second point, and an important qualifier. However less rigorous—in the theoretical sense—action research is, it is not for the careless or uncommitted. Because the findings are so context-specific, they may not be subject to the same level of outside scrutiny that a purely academic project might be. Ethically speaking, action research requires a great deal of internal scrutiny. Sloppy work can be damaging and is certainly unprofessional.

*Needs internal scrutiny*

What we are saying here is that the processes and outcomes of your site-based research project affect the lives and work of members of your organization and as such deserve the utmost care and attention. We believe that a caring and careful researcher—regardless of formal training—will take this responsibility seriously, learn what she needs to learn, and carry out whatever steps are necessary to be helpful and truthful in her work. We will examine these ideas more thoroughly when we look at research ethics in Chapter 3.

## Approaching Problems with Action Research

First and foremost, action research begins with a basic set of attitudes. These include:

- **Commitment.** Participants should be involved with the project for its duration and feel a personal investment in its successful completion.

- **Collaboration.** Action research is not for control freaks! Power relations among participants are equal, and all perspectives shape the "spirit" of the work.
- **Concern.** The interpretive nature of action research means participants must develop a supportive community of critical friends.
- **Consideration.** Action research assumes willingness to critically assess one's own motivations and behaviours with respect to the project. (This can be difficult but is ultimately rewarding!)
- **Change.** Action research encourages people to take risks and embrace possibilities.

Some of these attitudes may be quite uncharacteristic of more traditional organizations. For instance, the example of hierarchical action noted below is clearly not an example of the sort of negotiation that occurs naturally in action research; however, it is an example of change in a typical organization. The intent may be good, but the process is less than democratic. And from the practical point of view, it will generally not result in positive change.

## How Not to Solve a Problem

The president of a national corporation visits one of the regional offices and notices that morale in the office is very low. Most of the support staff are discouraged, and no one seems interested in the affairs of the company. She quickly calls a meeting with the local vice-president and the regional and district managers. They discuss the issue. One manager suggests that they stagger the morning and afternoon coffee breaks so that the support staff will have less opportunity to share negative feelings. This suggestion is implemented the following week. When the president returns to the office for another visit, it is clear that the situation has not improved. It has, in fact, deteriorated.

The approach chosen—staggering the coffee breaks—was reasonable, perhaps; however, it was not an effective way to deal with the problem. It just didn't help.

So now what? The first step would be to try to figure out the number of possible factors contributing to the problem of morale—or perhaps morale isn't even the problem. Next, it would be good to know why the attempt at solving the problem failed. As in many organizations, someone saw the issue and acted unilaterally. That's typical. Here, no one really took time to study the problem and determine the actual cause of the low morale. Specifically, management failed to take into account low wages, recent layoffs, and the resulting heavier-than-normal workload. We also know that support staff were not given an opportunity to voice their concerns or to participate in a solution. Once again, decisions were made without staff input and—guess what—the result was another downturn in morale. This is an example of a case where action research might be a helpful alternative.

## Conclusion

In this chapter, we've stressed the need for commitment in an action research project. Action research is a process that requires time, energy, and focus. Essentially, we believe (and have seen) action research accomplish great things in schools and other organizations we have worked with. However, as seems to be the case with most things in life that are worth doing, action research is more perspiration than inspiration. All research team members need to see the value of the project if they are to carry it through.

In conducting your own project, you will play a large role in explaining and generating support for the site-based research approach to problem solving. It is our hope that this chapter provides you with just the tools you need to do this.

Why would we be interested in doing this? Simply stated, we believe that research can and should result in improving the quality of human life and we want to be part of that change. We are educators—teachers—by vocation and profession; however, this does not mean that we believe our work is limited to schools. Neither of us can recall having any kind of a job—in education or outside education—that has not included learning. Every organization that hopes to expand and grow has an educative aspect. Workers need to learn how to learn, and—as politically incorrect as it might seem to say so these days—people do not already possess inside themselves all the information they need. People need to be taught. This does not mean taught from above by a hierarchical leader; it could be that one person on the job teaches another, and so on.

Remi DeRoo and the Canadian Catholic Bishops released a paper many years ago noting the rights of humans to good work. The bishops observed that after God created humans one of his gifts was work—naming the animals and tending the Garden of Eden. Good work also includes good human communication, an implicit place for the spirit, and a place for social gathering and human creation (perhaps the most joyous work).

We trust that your research project will allow you to expand your own support and commitment to others, and help you create your greatest project—yourself.

**Fig. 2.3. Origins of Action Research**

---

### Where Did Action Research Come From?

Action research orginated in the 1930s with the work of Kurt Lewin and was later adapted by educators to study classrooms. In the late 1950s, action research declined in prominence, but it has regained a pre-eminent position in social research. During the liberal and socially progressive 1960s and early 1970s, action research regained popularity and came to be seen as an inquiry done by practitioners with the help of an outside consultant. In the mid-1970s, the definition of action research began to expand to include the study of organizational practices.

Egalitarian principles further widened to incorporate the notion of **worker as researcher.** The idea here is that one needn't sit around and wait for "experts" to come in from the outside and offer solutions to organizational problems. It is a grassroots approach that validates and empowers the unique perspectives that come from average workers *within* the organization. It is assumed that caring and committed laypersons can initiate and carry out useful research that directly addresses their "felt" problems. An outside consultant, skilled in research practices, can offer guidance and coaching, but the emphasis is on collaborative construction of meanings.

Today, action research is being used by a large variety of people who work with organizations to plan and conduct research projects. A variety of models exist for planning and implementing action research projects. Some theorists distinguish traditional action research from critical emancipatory action research.

In **traditional action research**, practitioners/workers are viewed as active producers of knowledge, and action research projects are conducted to improve practice through a better understanding of the multiple layers of meaning and the fullness of institutional actions.

## Site-Based Research

We have explored a number of types and dimensions of research in general and action research in particular; now it is time to take a closer look at the type of research that will apply specifically to your own project work. Your project will draw on the principles of action research, but it may also differ from action research in significant ways.

Specifically, your project departs from what we can genuinely call "action research" in at least two ways. First, action research is characterized by a cycle of researching issues, implementing change, reflecting on outcomes, and then making adjustments before moving into another cycle of change and reflection. This recursive process will not necessarily be a feature of your project work. You *will* likely be studying an issue in your workplace, reporting on your findings, and perhaps making recommendations for change. However, without time to implement your recommendations, you won't necessarily be completing even one cycle. A full-cycle completion of a project is often a longer process than you have time for during this stage of your graduate work. The fully recursive cycle (as you would find in action research) is not a requirement of your site-based research work.

A second basic difference is that action research is explicitly democratic and participatory. Philosophically and practically, an objective of action research is to narrow or eliminate the gaps between researcher and researched. Typically, an action research project would pull an entire team of people together to explore issues, suggest action and possible solutions, and discuss the impact of any actions that are undertaken. During your research, you will probably be working more autonomously, although we do encourage you to take from the concepts of action research to build and sustain good relationships with your research subjects.

Whereas action research is something undertaken by a larger number of practitioners "on the job," your work, as part of a formal graduate degree program, for practical reasons necessitates that you assume a clear role as a single researcher and full responsibility for the conduct and outcomes of your work. Generally, you are working alone. You certainly may work with a colleague on a single site-based project, but usually your colleagues in graduate work live at different sites and co-research is difficult.

Because your project methodology departs from genuine action research in these significant ways, we refer to the study framework that will guide *your* work as **site-based research.** We have outlined the principles of action research because we believe in their efficacy. You are encouraged to adhere to the ethical and rigorous practice inherent in action research; however, we understand that it would be difficult, if not impossible, to employ all aspects specifically or fully during your graduate work.

The phrase *site-based research* was chosen based on our belief that your research should be applied in the context within which you work—based on an issue within your site. Recalling the distinctions between basic and applied research discussed in Chapter 1, both action research and our own site-based research approach fall into the category of *applied research*. That is, applied research can be addressed to specific circumstances. Such site-based research is largely qualitative in its approach and concerns itself with identifying and solving problems in real-world settings. Such settings include your organization, but could include any other organization as well. We have used the same principles to supervise the research work of teachers, police officers, corporate executives, health care practitioners, personal trainers, and civic planners, to name only a few.

The value of your site-based research is that many people really do have a vested interest in the work you will do. They care. What you do really is relevant and important to others. You will note later that we will ask you to disseminate your work widely—especially among those who share your interests and workplace. Hopefully, even after you complete your studies, your project will bring people together to make a positive change in your school or organization. Wherever it is undertaken, the goal of the site-based research you will undertake is to facilitate thoughtful, proactive problem solving. Dare we say, to make things better?

# THREE

**RESEARCH**
## *Ethics*

*As researchers, we must guard the well-being
of our participants.*

**CONDUCTING RESEARCH IS AN ENORMOUS RESPONSIBILITY.** Done well, research is a means to understand and ultimately improve upon the human condition. We can seek to develop effective instruction for adult English as a Second Language learners in China, study post-hospitalization adjustment in children with

Crohn's disease, learn about the nutritional needs of young children in a remote northern community, look for ways to enhance student physical activity during the school day, or enhance preventative programming at a local mental health clinic—to name just a few possibilities!

Done poorly, selfishly, or unethically, the same research efforts are at best ineffective—a waste of valuable time, energy, and resources—or at worst, can inflict lasting damage on an organization or group. Fortunately, truly disastrous violations of research ethics are fairly few and far between. More common are situations where badly conducted research results in hard feelings, embarrassments, inaccurate findings, or ineffective recommendations.

In graduate work, students are expected—to a greater or lesser extent—to enter the research community and hence assume the responsibility that comes with reading about, observing, and reporting on human activities. Clear ethical guidelines help ensure that we do this work well.

## The Importance of Research Ethics

Because we live in a democratic society, we seek principles in our research that are compatible with democratic ideals. In other words, we strive to protect the rights and freedoms of the participants who offer their time and information to further our work. In a general way, these participants are under our care, and if we were so inclined, we could misuse, reshape, or reinterpret information they give us in heinous ways. Even when researching adults, we must attend to democratic principles. We would not want it otherwise.

Researchers in the Western world thus adhere to democratic methods, such as:

*Widely sharing information and data*
- The study should be open to review and scrutiny by all those affected by the process.
- When decisions are made, evidence should be drawn from as wide a variety of sources as possible.

*Minimizing biases*

- Research methods should be used as impartially as possible. Research is an honest search for knowledge; it should not serve to support individual presuppositions or to address a researcher's vested interests.
- Research should be open-ended; the results should not be predetermined.
- Because different research methods may reveal different data (we call this *triangulation*), when appropriate, different methods should be used to gain other data perspectives.

*Sharing self-scrutiny and corrective actions in the research process*

- Where needed, when reporting research results researchers should share insights and evolutions in their thinking.
- Researchers should tell others who might follow their research what was not found and speculate honestly about why it was not found. If it was their fault, they should admit it.
- Researchers should report any problems with methods of data collection.

In short, as a researcher you should make every effort to be open about your intentions, honest with your participants, and fair in your representation of the situation and issue you are studying. If most of this sounds like common sense, that's because it is. Few students we've met ever set out to conduct their research in a *dis*honest or *un*fair fashion! Instead, sometimes ethically sticky issues may catch students off guard, but in our experience, most problems can be avoided when the researcher approaches the research with care, attention, and sensitivity to his participants and organization. Some of the most common issues we've seen arise are presented below.

## *Managing Sensitive Information*

A specific problem occurs when participants share information off the record. Sometimes participants just love to talk—perhaps to show they are in the know. These people may even reveal an organization member's involvement in illegal activities, abuse, or other destructive behaviours. Confessions like these present dilemmas for a researcher who has offered confidentiality (Creswell 1998). Our rule of thumb is that if you don't want to take responsibility for an answer, don't ask the question. When encountering unrequested and unwanted information, it is acceptable to steer the conversation in another direction and, if necessary, to politely inform the person you are speaking with that what he or she is sharing creates ethical difficulties for your work.

Another potential source of problems arises once you begin to record information. All data must be stored properly and carefully, and the researcher must ensure that data are viewed only by those with permission to do so. In short, it is difficult to be too cautious.

Finally, the data you collect will eventually have to be reported. Obviously you do not want to undermine the breadth of your study's findings by ignoring anything unpleasant, but you may want to consider in advance how you might best frame sensitive material. One student we know made an early commitment to all participants in his research study that all of his findings would be shared openly. What was he to do when critical comments about one teacher arose? There were no names mentioned, yet given the size of the school, all staff would know on whom these negative statements centred—and probably who had made them.

## Protecting Your Research Participants

Research ethics typically means treating human research participants in accordance with the "rules" of research. For example, participants give permission for researchers to seek data from them. To make certain that participants are protected from harm, participants are traditionally allowed to quit a research project at any time for any reason. Because the data they give researchers can be potentially problematic, they are also allowed protection by staying—if they choose—anonymous.

In all research, the methodology chosen to conduct the study must be considerate. Researchers are almost always in a position of power with regard to their participants. Can you imagine the damage that research gossip could do to a participant who, by honestly answering a researcher's questions, reveals too much or uses wording that another person might find offensive?

People are usually less sensitive about what they say about others and more sensitive about what others say about them. People also tend to be sensitive about things they really care about. Researchers must always remember and consider their potential power to do harm. We are not paparazzi; we are scholars. Issues to be considered include confidentiality, protecting participants from harm, and providing informed consent. Researchers must be trustworthy, and they must hold the information they gain in confidence. As researchers, we ask much of our participants, and we must be good gatekeepers. This means we must consider the ethical impact of our talk and our actions.

## *Doing Your Research Well*

There is another sense of research ethics that we seldom discuss: that of conducting the research well. Or, as Laura explains it, there is research that doesn't do any harm per se, but doesn't do much good either. Good research is worth doing.

Research should be an ethical in two ways: first, the questions researchers ask should be "good" questions—they should be valuable inquiries, not trivial. Second, researchers hold the public trust; they should therefore, as an act of will, work hard to do research well. If researchers do not attend to these two activities—asking valuable questions and holding trust—they trivialize their research participants and those who support their research activities.

This begs the central question How can research be done well? Implied in this question is the fact that not all researchers have done research honestly or with consideration for others—either their research participants or the institutions in which their research has been conducted. Sadly, those who live within a research community can relate to tears shed in the wake of thoughtless or inconsiderate research projects. For example, one researcher entered a study of a school already having *decided* that racism was rampant within the school she was studying. To no one's surprise, she found rampant racism. The old saying that you find what you look for is as true in research as in life.

*More than minimal risk occurs when the possible harms implied by the subjects' participation in the research could go beyond those encountered in those aspects of the subjects' everyday life.*

It is also true that researchers sometimes conduct their research ignorant of established practices and as a result have gathered findings that proved worthless for organizational change. For instance, one focus group researcher asked each focus group specific questions about the topic rather than providing a general focus for the research. She also relied on summary notes written by a secretary instead of transcriptions of group conversations, never realizing that the research findings were "confounded" because her specific questions controlled the group's discussion. Furthermore, she missed the chance to explore the topic widely and her already compromised findings were further problematic because they were limited to what her secretary had decided was important enough to note. Who knows what research findings became faded background noise?

Action research—and its variation as site-based research—is, fundamentally, a human search to gather information that improves life. It is also an accepted way of making organizational changes that encourage positive practices and help to eliminate negative ones. Research is a valuable activity—worth doing well.

## Fig. 3.1. Specific Ethical Issues of a Site-Based Research Project

Patricia Dugan and Mary-Beth Reid designed a site-based research project in 2000 called "Women and the Chain of Command." Their research focused on women who were working their way towards senior leadership levels in traditionally male-dominated fields. The purpose of the study was:

- to organize and lead a group of women entrepreneurs through a change process
- to understand the personal characteristics and organizational patterns that aided the advancement of women to decision-making levels
- to build on factors of success
- to provide action plans that help remove barriers and enhance women's leadership in all aspects of society.

One major ethical consideration was confidentiality. The women in the research group needed to share their thoughts and feelings in a safe environment. Many were uncomfortable sharing what they believed to be more male-oriented desires like their dreams of status and getting ahead. They were concerned their organizational and psychological positions would be jeopardized.

The researchers and the participants agreed that the content of discussions and the membership list would remain confidential until they concluded their work together. Once the work was finished, the researchers believed participants would feel a sense of freedom. In the meantime, creating this private space would encourage honest and open sharing of information.

# Ethics and Your Organization

Recently, a friend told us about a disconcerting experience with a visitor at her house. Jane was playing a CD and preparing a meal for her guests when one of them came in with her own case of CDs and asked, "Hey, do you mind if I change the music?" Not wanting to make waves, Jane agreed, but shared with us how uncomfortable it was to have a guest coming into her home and calling the shots without being invited to do so.

Of course most of us, like Jane, would find this presumptuous houseguest a bit of a pain. We want visitors to respect our spaces and "the way we do things around here." Researchers extend the same respect by ensuring that their research conduct within an organization or institution coincides with established codes of ethics. The process of site-based research must not violate principals an organization has previously established as an ethical base.

You should, therefore, consult any ethical statements provided by your organization. Not only is this right from an ethical standpoint, it can also serve to sensitize you to the climate in which you will be working. A statement of ethics may well reveal some of what is important to the organization and hence provide clues about what aspects of its management and relationships might bear more scrutiny on your part.

Following are sample statements of ethics from two organizations. What does each reveal about the organization's mandate and values? As a researcher, what special area(s) should you probably attend to carefully?

**Example 1.** The Australian Advertising Federation produced in 2002 a statement of ethics that defines the values and principles at the heart of what its members stand for in advertising. They promise to:

- work to deserve trust in all relationships
- honour agreements
- promote a climate of open communication
- uphold both the spirit and letter of the law
- respect the essential dignity of all people
- treat people fairly
- give due weight to all considered criticism, including contravention of these values

- let a well-informed conscience resolve a conflict of interest or principles
- be aware that acting as the client's agent carries additional responsibilities to acting as vendor to the client
- give our best work
- give good value and service
- provide a rewarding work environment
- work to built the integrity of the industry
- compete fairly
- recognize that our craft gives us an opportunity to make a positive contribution to people's lives and society's values
- challenge directives that appear to be against the community interest
- be responsible in the portrayal of race, age, disability, gender, sexual orientation, and religion
- be mindful of the credulity and potential vulnerability of children who do not understand commercial intent.

– ADVERTISING FEDERATION OF AUSTRALIA 2002

**Example 2.** Another example of a statement of ethics is provided by the Better Business Bureau of Mainland British Columbia. In business practices, its members are expected to demonstrate:

- **equality** – recognizing the individual rights of all community members (in accord with the Canadian Charter of Rights and Freedoms) and treating people justly
- **truth** – making accurate claims to customers, using only competent testimonials, and striving to be open about all aspects of the products or services
- **honesty** – upholding the principle of fair play and vigilantly opposing conduct that has the intent, capability, or effect of being deceptive
- **integrity** – not merely abiding by the law in a technical way, but striving to serve customers with honest values, avoiding all devices and schemes which prey on human ignorance or gullibility
- **cooperativeness** – supporting a healthy marketplace for all through cooperation with customers, other businesses, and all who would benefit from an ethical, free-market system

- **self-regulation** – honouring all commitments and guarantees, and seeking to resolve disputes in a fair, expeditious manner. This includes investigating and striving to eliminate and fully inform the customer of any health, safety, environmental, or other hazards posed by the normal use of a product or service.

– BETTER BUSINESS BUREAU 2000

**Fig. 3.2. Reflective Questions for Ethical Researchers**

---

**Reflective Questions**

As a researcher, it is helpful to consider examples of ethical questions that inform your site-based research project. The following questions are fruitful to consider as you progress through your project.

- How might intended changes from your project affect others?
- Who has an interest in being informed about your project?
- Who will own the information generated by the project?
- How does the project express an ethic of caring for others?
- In whose interest is the change you propose being made?
- Who will own the success/failure of the project?

– ACTION RESEARCH GUIDE FOR ALBERTA TEACHERS, 2000

---

# University Research Ethics Policy

Canadian universities conduct research according to the guidelines set out by the Tri-Council Policy Statement, a "mega-code of ethics" established by Canada's three major research granting bodies to govern research conducted on humans (Palys 2003). These guidelines determine safe, appropriate, ethical, and fair conduct of scholarly research, and they are used by ethics review boards to approve research projects.

It is a good idea to be familiar with the basics of these guidelines as you approach your research design. We have condensed this information to hit the aspects we consider most relevant.

## Ethics Review Required

An ethics review is required when research involves data collected from human subjects. This data collection includes:

- Information collected from living humans through interaction (interviews, questionnaires, surveys, and focus groups) or through intervention (if the subject is affected by being placed in a situation that will be studied).
- Secondary non-public sources that identify an individual. (Secondary sources, in this instance, do not refer to public secondary sources such as books, monographs, and articles.) Sources include:

  - information gathered by another researcher for another purpose that identifies an individual; for example, interviews about an individual.
  - information gathered by the researcher for another purpose that identifies an individual; for example, information from a private database such as one connected to a school that includes private information.

- Naturalistic observation used to study subjects' behaviour in a natural environment. The Tri-Council Policy states: "Because knowledge of the research can be expected to influence behaviour, naturalistic observation generally implies that the subjects do not know that they are being observed, and hence can not have given their free and informed consent."

## When Ethics Reviews Are Not Required

Some research involving humans does not require review and approval by an ethics review committee:

- Research about a living individual involved in the public area, or about an artist, based exclusively on publicly available information
- Quality assurance studies, performance reviews, or testing within normal educational requirements (however, when such information is used as a secondary non-public source, an ethical review may be required)
- Research involving only observation in public settings (as opposed to naturalistic observation) where it is expected that participants are seeking public visibility (for example, a rally or a public meeting)

- Research involving information from public databases where aggregated information cannot be associated with an individual or specific group
- Research involving human subjects conducted by academic faculty or staff as "outside professional activity"
- Research undertaken by university students outside of the auspices of the university
- Research already in the public domain, such as autobiographies or public archives (as opposed to non-public secondary sources noted in the section above).

## Guiding Ethical Principles

Research activity should conform to the following principles as set out in the Tri-Council Policy Statement "Ethical Conduct for Research Involving Humans" (1997):

- Respect for human dignity
- Respect for free and informed consent
- Respect for vulnerable persons
- Respect for privacy and confidentiality
- Respect for justice and inclusiveness.

## Balancing Harms and Benefits

To warrant participation of human subjects, researchers and their ethics review committee must consider the benefits of the research in relation to the participants, the researcher, organizations or communities that may be directly involved, the academic community, and society.

**Estimate of risk.** The Tri-Council Policy Statement offers the following explanation for *minimal risk*: "If the potential subjects can reasonably be expected to regard the probability and magnitude of possible harms implied by participation in the research to be no greater than those encountered in those aspects of his or her everyday life that relate to the research, then the research can be regarded as within the range of minimal risk."

*You will be proud of your "baby"*
*when you have endured the "labour" of your research.*

Conversely, risk that is more than minimal occurs when the possible harms implied by participation in the research could exceed those encountered in related aspects of the subject's everyday life; for example, this could involve any risks relating to confidentiality, vulnerable populations such as children, or psychological stress.

### Requirement for Free and Informed Consent

The Tri-Council Policy Statement underscores the great importance of free and informed consent in ethical research involving human subjects. Research may begin only when prospective subjects (or authorized third parties) have been given an opportunity to provide free and informed consent about their partici- pation. The researcher must make it clear to subjects that they may withdraw at any point in the research study. Free and informed consent is given voluntarily without undue influence.

Ordinarily, free and informed consent will be given in writing. Where informed consent in writing is not culturally appropriate, or where other good reasons exist for not obtaining written consent, the researcher must document the alternative procedures used to indicate free and informed consent.

The requirement to obtain informed consent may be waived or modified with research in which the following conditions can be documented (in accordance with the Tri-Council Policy Statement):

- The waiver or modification is unlikely to affect the welfare of the subjects.
- The research involves no more than minimal risk.
- The research could not be practically carried out without a waiver or modification.
- The waiver or modification does not involve therapeutic intervention.
- The subjects are provided with additional information and, where possible and appropriate, provided with additional pertinent information after the study.
- If the research incorporates randomization or blind clinical trials, and if the subjects are informed of the probability of being randomly assigned to a category, such research is not regarded as a waiver or alteration of the requirements for consent.

**Informing potential subjects.** The researcher should provide subjects with information that invites them to participate in the research, a statement outlining the research purpose, the identity of the researcher, the research procedures, the length of the participation, an indication of how the research findings will be used, and additional pertinent information where relevant.

**Competence.** The Tri-Council Policy Statement identifies three conditions for recruiting individuals who are not legally competent as subjects.

1. Free and informed consent will be requested from an authorized representative who may speak for the person.
2. Only people in the identified group will be asked the research questions.
3. The research does not exceed minimal risk.

## Privacy and Confidentiality

Privacy and confidentiality refer to all aspects of the access, control, and dissemination of information derived from the subjects. When a subject volunteers information, the researcher has an obligation to not share that information with others unless there is free and informed consent. The researcher should clearly indicate to the subject the degree to which confidentiality can be expected. The Tri-Council Policy Statement indicates that anonymity is generally the best protection of the confidentiality of personal information and records.

Approval by a research ethics board for the interview procedure is required when researchers plan to access identifiable personal information through personal interviews (face-to-face, telephone, electronic, or other). Board approval is also required for accessing private information through surveys, questionnaires, and the collection of data. The researcher shall provide information on the type and purpose of data to be collected, limits on use and disclosure, modes of observation that identify individuals, safeguards for confidentiality and for security of information, possible links between the data gathered for the research, and other personal or public records.

## Secondary Use of Data
If data from records collected for a purpose other than the proposed research (i.e., secondary data) can be linked to individuals and there is a possibility that individuals could be identified in published reports, ethics board approval is required.

## Inclusion
Within the ethics framework, *inclusion* refers to the overall benefits and burdens of research being distributed fairly. No one group should be asked to bear an unfair burden of research. Consideration should also be given to the potential for members of society to be unfairly excluded from the benefits of the research.

## Research Involving Aboriginal Peoples
The Tri-Council Policy Statement treats Aboriginal peoples as a special group and recognizes that research involving Aboriginal individuals might also involve the community to which they belong. It recognizes the importance of documents specifically relevant to Aboriginal peoples (prepared by the Royal Commission on Aboriginal Peoples, the Association of Canadian Universities for Northern Studies, and the Inuit Circumpolar Conference). These documents identify acceptable practices for research with Aboriginal communities.

When conducting research with Aboriginal persons, researchers must consider the interests of the Aboriginal group when describing the group, when subjects speak on behalf of an Aboriginal group, when leaders of a group identify potential subjects, and when information or property belonging to the group as a whole is researched.

## Conclusion

Exhibiting ethics in research could be as simple as knowing what not to do and promising, in writing, not to do it. Many universities seem to shape research ethics into a duty—perhaps not one a researcher embraces, but one that a researcher is required to fulfill. Such an attitude is understandable but sad. Research ethics involve both the law and the heart.

Legally, universities can and have gotten into trouble by playing fast and loose with participants, and laws are created and enforced so that researchers "do no harm." The heart, however, requires that we go beyond doing no harm and actively seek to do good. Rather than treating participants like passive and powerless subjects in the medieval sense, we engage them as partners in our quest to discover or create research knowledge that shapes and improves practice.

Recently, some universities have begun to formally recognize this proactive philosophy by including the word *integrity* alongside the concept of ethics. Researching with integrity—doing good work well—is, to us, a solid part of any full definition of research ethics.

In short, researchers come in all flavours. But to our minds, the best researchers set out to do good research studies as well as they are able. They work with sincerity and consideration. They protect their participants. And they share the knowledge they create or discover as widely and as sagaciously as they can. They see their work as adding to the collective understandings of a community of people who care about improving the lives of others and who will do whatever possible to act on that principle. Being a researcher is a vocation that makes a difference.

# FOUR

# *Planning*
## YOUR RESEARCH PROJECT

*Before you begin your research, you should clearly state the purpose
of the research, identify the researcher, describe the research
procedures and time requirements, and prepare a statement
of how your findings will be used.*

**A COMMON REFLECTION WE HEAR FROM GRADUATE STUDENTS** about theses or
capping projects is how daunting the process seems in the early stages. No
matter how many research papers are completed in earlier classes, students see
the stakes go up when they hit their final big research project. It is one thing to
hang out in databases and synthesize existing academic literature into a paper
whose only audience is a professor; it is another thing entirely to take responsibility for a process that involves and affects real people in a real organization.

One insight we can offer you is this: people can and do successfully complete site-based research projects. Laura compares it to childbirth (Jim just can't quite relate to this).

> I hit this stage in my pregnancy where I was genuinely terrified of labour. "This is gonna hurt!"
>
> Yet when I looked down at my belly, I realized that the outcome was pretty inevitable. The baby was going to come out whether I liked it or not. I also realized that all of the women I knew had survived labour and come out quite comfortably on the other side of it. If it had been done successfully so many times before, certainly I could do it too! This was a great source of comfort for me.

So we can comfortably assure you that the process is doable, and you will be proud of your baby when you have endured the labour of your research. The key is (and this may sound trite, but it's true) to take one step at a time, and one of the goals of this book is to lead you—as simply and clearly as possible—through the necessary steps.

The steps of our site-based research model, as presented here and in the following chapters, are a composite of various theoretical models of field-based research processes and Jim's experience working with scores of graduate students since the early 1970s. Again, we look primarily at action research to lend understanding to the general approach you will take in your site-based project.

## The Action Research Process

There are many perspectives and models published on the process of action research, and we will share a brief description of several authors' views. In doing this, we hope to offer you a sense of how inclusive and flexible this methodology can be. While some faculties of graduate studies take our broad view in defining action research, there are proponents who feel that there is only one correct way. As we have stated earlier, we believe any research that promises action and improvement within an organization is acceptable, as long as it's ethical, helpful, and done well. We believe that action research and site-based research provide an optimum way for educators to make applied and lasting changes to the places where they live and work.

## An Action and Reflection Spiral

In more traditional interpretations, action research is viewed as a cyclical or spiral process that moves from reflection to action and back to reflection again. An action research project may have one or many iterations of a planning-action-evaluation process; oftentimes, it even lacks a definite outcome! In fact, in many models, action research is viewed not as an isolated project, but as an ongoing *philosophy* of thinking, learning, and organizational problem solving.

**Fig. 4.1. The action research planning process.**

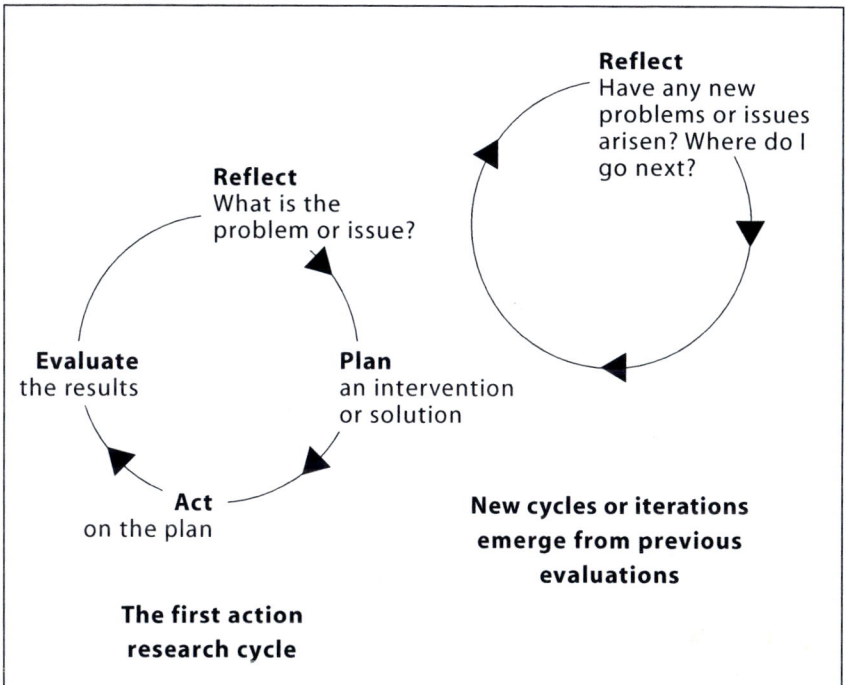

Reflect
Have any new problems or issues arisen? Where do I go next?

Reflect
What is the problem or issue?

Evaluate
the results

Plan
an intervention or solution

Act
on the plan

New cycles or iterations emerge from previous evaluations

The first action research cycle

This ongoing, re-cycling process may appear odd when many of us are so conditioned to solve problems in a linear fashion, concluding in a definite resolution. However, if we reflect a bit on the existing problems and relationships that characterize our lives, we quickly realize that problems are rarely solved in this linear way. Why? First, our problems are often difficult to define. Second, there is rarely one clear and obvious solution. Third, once resolved, issues tend to be far from over and will flow into new sorts of problems and opportunities.

All the while, the process is witnessed and negotiated by different stakeholders with different values and perspectives. You may not read this in another book about research, but we believe that action research is primarily about relationships: relationships between people and people, between people and knowledge, between doing and thinking about doing. Action research recognizes that life's problems (and their solutions) are messy business. So, we impose some order with a methodology, but we remain flexible enough to accommodate what we learn. The following models are examples of action research methodologies that provide an overall direction and shape for a project without being too restrictive. You can use these general frameworks to think about the big picture in your own site-based project.

## Action Research Model No. 1: Ernest Stringer

Similar to much work in this field, our work draws on that of Ernest T. Stringer, who is generally regarded as a current guru of action research. Stringer (1999) offers a methodology which can be constructed as a basic approach to or routine for action research. The process is simple and flexible enough to adapt to any personally directed action research project that might be designed.

His definitions (and our own) also imply processes that demand participation and negotiation from those within an organization. In other words, you are not working alone on your research project; you must consider the needs and desires of your partners and stakeholders. Such a research position (and there is no contradiction here) calls for both flexibility and rigorous work.

Here is Stringer's process.

### Step 1: Look
- Gather relevant information. (Gather data.)
- Build a picture that describes the situation. (Define and describe.)

### Step 2: Think
- Explore and analyze: "What is happening here?" (Analyze.)
- Interpret and explain: "How and why are things the way they are?" (Theorize.)

*Step 3: Act*
- Plan. (Report.)
- Implement and evaluate. (Act and report.)

This step-by-step process may be deceptively linear in its appearance, but recall the spiralling nature of the work. For Stringer, action research is an interacting, recycling spiral, within which the researcher is constantly looking back and reflecting upon what he has already done. This reflection informs and generates new actions.

Gummesson (2000) adds a second spiral to his hermeneutic circle. In this process, new understandings are developed and reconsidered naturally as new information comes to light. The process is iterative; in other words, each stage of the work becomes part of an action research project.

To explain it differently, we always begin a new study with *pre-understandings* about the research. An advanced understanding may be as simple as knowing that you chose a subject you knew and cared about. Think about it: you could not have chosen a subject that you had absolutely no knowledge of. So accept that you started your project at a place of some knowledge and experience. And as your project progresses, it makes sense that you will learn more about it. In fact, the act of working through a research project takes on its own process and levels of understanding. Each level is different from those previous, yet built from the knowledge gained in earlier activities.

To gain a sense of how this pre-understanding works, read this autobiographical statement by E. B. White, author of the popular children's novel *Charlotte's Web*. White explains how the story evolved from his own knowledge and personal experiences:

> Writing for children is usually regarded as a separate form of madness. I came to it by accident and stayed with it when it proved to be much like other kinds of writing—hard work, followed by pleasing rewards. The character Stuart Little appeared to me in a dream one night when I was traveling by rail. A writer is always grateful for small favours and I recall that I jotted down fragments of the tale next morning. I had no intention of writing a book for children, however, and the thing merely grew, by slow stages, over a period of about twelve years....

As for *Charlotte's Web*, it came about as a result of my close association with animals in a barn. This barn, with its creatures and its swallows, has always been a place where I have felt at peace, and I deliberately tried to bring it to life in a story for youngsters. Many of the characters are taken right from life, including the pig and the spider. The tragedy of animal death by murder, which always haunts a farm, haunted me and I guess I was trying to write my way out of the dilemma in the story of Charlotte.... (HW Wilson Co., 1963)

Like White, we must be comfortable starting with a scrap of an idea and working with a bit of uncertainty and serendipity in the creative process—only here we are creating research instead a children's story. Stephen Covey's seemingly sage advice in *The Seven Habits of Highly Effective People* (1989)—"Begin with the end in mind"—just does not work here. We know many graduate students who want to see everything before they begin anything. Perhaps they fear they will not be able to control the process. Who knows? But they get stuck in the starting block because they simply cannot see the end they are searching for.

In action research, you are always venturing into the unknown, and you will find yourself in much the same position in your site-based research project. You simply cannot control and understand everything that will happen. As you work, be rigorous, be wise, and be ethical. But, like in the 1989 Steven Spielberg movie *Indiana Jones and the Last Crusade* when Harrison Ford steps out over the abyss into what seems like nothingness, sometimes you just "gotta go for it." (But not without thinking! Don't forget how to decide which cup to drink from when you get there.)

### Action Research Model No. 2: Jeffrey Glanz

In his book *Action Research: An Educational Leader's Guide to School Improvement* (1998), Jeffrey Glanz describes another way to process action research.

**Select a focus.** For Glanz, selecting a focus includes three steps:

1. Decide what you want to investigate
2. Develop a series of questions about the area you've chosen
3. Establish a plan to answer the question.

As you focus on a problem, pose beginning questions that will guide your research. Developing a series of guiding questions eventually leads to the specific research questions that will organize your study. Selecting a focus also includes developing initial research methodology. At this stage, the research methodology may simply include a simple series of what-to-do steps.

**Collect your data.** Once you have developed a workable research project—one that attends to the improvement of an organizational problem (or an opportunity to gain more knowledge about your organization)—it is time to begin collecting your data. As you work, use a variety of methods to provide evidence of the effectiveness of your intervention. Methods may include tests, surveys, interviews, or the examination of relevant documents.

Immerse yourself in the work. Remember that any data you collect must be transformed into a usable form. The best definition of "usable form" is a form that both (1) tells you what you need to know, and (2) allows you to clearly explain the information to others in your final report.

**Analyze and interpret your findings.** Once relevant data have been collected, begin to analyze and interpret what you have. What do your data mean? What interventions or opportunities can be proposed based upon what you have learned? Your goal here is to represent your findings in a clear and meaningful manner for others, and to generate feasible next steps for the organization you are studying.

**Take action based on your findings.** Because manageability is an issue, your site-based research stops at the point of actually implementing a possible intervention. However, where traditional action research includes testing the intervention, the concept of **grounded theory** becomes all the more important. A theory is "grounded" when your research questions are answered based on the data you collect and any decisions made are based upon the findings of your research project.

In simple words, the decisions you make must be shown as logical from the data that logically encouraged you to make them. You didn't make the stuff up; you can point to the data that led you to the finding—the footprint on the ground! Were you not to utilize or trust your findings, there would be no reason to conduct the research. Your organizational decision-making would be based on trial and error—and unconsidered trial and error at that.

Most action researchers note three possible choices you might make as you evaluate an action research project. These are quite obvious, though people seldom choose the second option. You may choose to:

1. Continue the intervention
2. Call it off—disband the intervention
3. Modify the intervention in ways that make sense based on what you have learned.

As you can see, action researchers can take any number of paths to accomplish the goals of the research. Upon choosing your overall design process, you will naturally be motivated to break the design into active steps.

## Planning Your Site-Based Research Project

The action research models above, though somewhat different, all begin with an attempt to gain a clear understanding of the problem or issue at hand. Your site-based project should begin with this step as well. This early focus is important: without it, your research can grow into a huge quagmire of unconnected data. Some care and attention towards defining your research issue at these early stages will make it much easier in the later stages when you want to organize your data into something that tells the "story" of an organizational problem and its possible resolutions.

### Choosing a Research Topic

It is possible in the early stages that you do not have a clue what you want to study. Some students come into a graduate research process with a clear sense of the types of problems or issues that interest them, but many are very uncertain at the outset. One reason is that many of us are not experienced (or for that matter terribly confident) with an authoritative approach to problem solving.

Your comfort level may depend on how much research responsibility you have carried in the past. If you are new to organizing a research study, do not be discouraged; in fact, the entire exercise of conducting graduate-level research will build your confidence more than you can imagine! One of Jim's favourite sayings is that there are two projects in every research project: (1) the project of gaining knowledge about what is being studied, and (2) the growth of the researcher doing the study. If you do your project well, you will gain both experience and knowledge. We can almost guarantee that you will see your organization—and very possibly the whole world outside of it—with new, critical eyes. This growing is actually quite exciting!

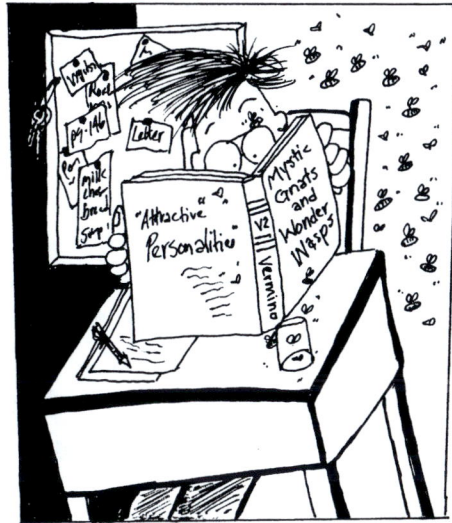

*You have chosen a topic, but you haven't quite decided how you will conduct your research....*

One way you can stimulate your thinking towards defining a topic (and gain some practice in your observation and fieldwork skills) is to actively assume the role of an observer. Because being an observer may be difficult in the context in which you work every day, one strategy is to begin to observe in an unfamiliar context. Try to select a context that might complement research in your own organization; for instance, you might observe another school or an organization you are not wholly familiar with. If you are a teacher, try observing another teacher's class. If you have occasion to visit a hospital, watch what happens in that ward. If you work with seniors in a health care setting, try observing a group of seniors in a recreational setting. As you have coffee in the mall, watch what happens around you.

You probably get the idea here: the trick is to choose a setting that has elements both familiar and unfamiliar to you. As you make your observations, you'll probably find yourself comparing and contrasting what you see with what you already know. In other words, you will begin to experience the subtle, critical work of a qualitative researcher. This work simultaneously recognizes what is known and what is new. It is open-ended and inquisitive work that is metacognitive in that the researcher is aware of herself, her subjects, and her surroundings. The skills you practise in these early stages will serve you well when you move into the heart of your actual research project—the collection of your data.

Another strategy for defining a project is simple brainstorming. The idea here is just to "play around." Keep a journal of your workday for a couple of weeks, and review it to see what themes may be emerging. Or try to free-write a list of questions without editing yourself. Sketch diagrams or graphic representations of your ideas and thoughts. Read a book about work, surf the internet, or play around in a database and key in search terms just to see what pops up.

Again, this is important work; these are skills you will use in later stages of your research project. Stay loose and open here—the ideas will come if you "play" consciously for a couple of weeks.

## Defining Your Question

Hopefully, through past experience or during some of the exercises we have described above, you will develop a sense of the process involved in defining a research question—and it is most certainly a process. Rarely is an issue or problem completely clear from the outset. To define the problem you will be addressing in your own research project, we recommend the following steps.

**Study your surroundings.** Take notes about the physical geography of the context. Watch how people live and work within that context. Ask and answer a series of simple, usually-taken-for-granted questions about the context of the place or organization in which your study will be conducted. One tenet of good qualitative research is stated in the phrase "seeing the unseen." We become so accustomed to the behaviour and communication patterns we experience every day that we cease to notice them. Your job is to see these patterns in fresh perspective.

**Identify a problem or area of concern.** Make certain—as certain as possible—that this is a real problem, not a chimera of a problem. You may find it difficult to build the cooperative relationships you need to complete your project if no one shares your belief that the issue you've identified is important. We encourage you to find and talk with a critical friend (and others if possible) about what you see. Coffee (or some coffee substitute) and conversation are priceless when thinking through a problem.

Remember, however, not everyone cares about your "neat" research problem. Don't wear the wrong friend out!

**Consider the problem.** Twist the problem around in different ways inside your head. Get your head around it, through it, and between it. Don't dwell on it in the front of your head; put it somewhere in the close background of your thoughts. Live with it like a comfortable friend. Consider it lightly when you drive and walk. It will reveal itself to you in comfort, not in stress. Do your work, but NEVER panic.

**Gather your team.** Collect a group of people who are interested in solving the problem or issue you have identified. See this as a social community of like-minded people, all committed to working with each other towards a solution. Have informal (rather than formal) agendas—don't ruin a good time by micromanaging it!

**Develop a suitable project and go with where it leads you.** Remember that you cannot know everything from the beginning. These projects take shape as you work. Be prepared to fly by the seat of your pants. Expect to tweak your methods. Don't get stressed over changes. If you do your work well without taking shortcuts or going cheap on the study's energy, chances are that you will make the correct choices. There are many right answers.

Remember that you have a project supervisor, critical friends among your graduate cohort, and work colleagues to support you. Use the skills and insights of your supporters, and listen to their thoughts. Too many people listen only a bit and then argue, trying to explain why they did this and that. Listen to constructive criticism and feedback with a basic assumption of trust. If you can't find this trust with the research friends you've got, find new research friends.

## The Importance of Description

As we have earlier noted, qualitative research is highly descriptive in nature. A clear understanding of the problem's context and stakeholders is critical—both for your own understanding and that of your readers. In terms of your project, the process of describing your project so that others can understand it will go a long way in helping you to keep your objectives in focus as you gather and interpret your data.

Therefore, once you have identified the problem or issue you wish to study, take time to describe it accurately. Some of these questions may guide your thinking and writing.

- Who is affected by the problem?
- Why do or should they care?
- What relationship dynamics might be contributing to the problem? What communication patterns do you observe?
- What contextual aspects are contributing? Pedagogical? Relational? Financial? Physical?
- How do stakeholders describe the problem? Outsiders?
- Think about conversations that you have participated in or witnessed. What do they tell you?
- Sometimes what is *not* said holds essential information—and is often of equal importance to what is said. What does the *un*spoken or *un*acknowledged tell you?
- Observe the behaviours and actions of those around you. What does their body language tell you?

# Considering Context

We keep mentioning the personal and unique nature of an action or site-based research study. We often hear people say, "I can't do that study. It's been done before." This is simply untrue! If two different people actually tried to do the same exact study, they simply couldn't pull it off. (Think of the recent remake of the movie *Psycho*.) The way each researcher interpreted the data would be vastly different. Nor could they write the report in the same way. We are all both captured and freed by our personal insights, and each of us, in the realm of our own site-based research projects, will produce unique research outcomes.

One thing contributing to this uniqueness is that each and every study has its own context. A project is conducted in a particular place, at a particular time, and with particular participants. A small room differs from a large room. Older people differ from teenagers. Men differ from women. Canadians differ from Americans. These differences must be taken into consideration. To help others understand your work, you need to tell them as much about the study's context as you can—all the time while ethically protecting participants. The better picture a reader has of your research setting, the more your research study makes sense.

## *Context and Your Organization*

Often research can shed light on unseen and seldom deconstructed contexts. Cultures exist and operate within all organizations, and many of their aspects are not readily apparent. If you consider your own experiences of becoming encultured into the places you've worked, you will probably realize that some of those lessons learned were not in the company handbook. Lessons might have included discovering where the rules were flexible and where they weren't, whether the organization was open or resistant to new ideas, which departments were "happy" places to be and which were not, and in which staff room you could find carrot muffins for Wednesday morning coffee. We might call this getting a feel for an organization. An insider's perspective, developed over time, embodies many aspects of organizational culture that are not apparent to outsiders.

On the other hand, an organization's insiders have their own blind spots. If you are studying your own organization, there may be aspects of its culture that you have never questioned or deconstructed. Perhaps you will not realize these nuances—and in some cases hazard zones—until you walk across the wrong lawns.

**Sample study.** *Edna completed an engaging site-based research project within her own health care organization. Her report was, to her mind, comprehensive and complete. However, her boss—who had worked within the organization for many years—believed that the report should follow a more traditional, quantitative reporting format and style. He said, "That's the way we do it in health care. If you don't write it this way, they won't take it seriously. In fact, they won't even read it." Edna considered her boss's point and realized he was right. She decided to tailor her final report to the specific audience for whom she was writing.*

Edna's supervisor wisely recommended that she attend to her organization's culture. If you are in the health care profession, you may already know that you may be dealing with a group of people who—either through personal hard-wiring or their own learning experiences—function in a world of quantitative research. They may find your site-based research project too qualitative for their tastes. They continue to believe one can replicate a study, that there can be research neutrality, and that you should do it their way. They are bothered by the fact that action research is often written in the first person and as a story. And as you work through your major project, you may find yourself working with a supervisor who is more in tune with traditional research methods and reporting styles. What do you do? The answer is that, in the tradition of action research, you negotiate your decisions with that person.

In some organizations, once you have obtained approval to do your research, you will face few restrictions. In other organizations, however, even if you receive official approval, your supervisor may place certain demands upon your reporting, limit your access to people or documents during your data collection, or request other modifications to your work. That's the way culture works, and while it can be frustrating to make such adjustments, ultimately your work will not be useful to the organization unless it matches existing norms and values.

## Fig. 4.2. A Teacher Leader Considers Context

A social studies department head in a suburban high school had been struggling for the past year to implement collaborative practices among her colleagues. Her predecessor, who had since retired, had implemented a "community of practice" model that asked staff to develop and act upon a core mission statement. Scheduling had been adjusted to provide the staff with more time to work together. Yet meetings had broken down. Three teachers had developed a good collaborative working relationship as a result of the regular meeting times and taken full advantage of the opportunities these presented, but the rest of the department staff had drifted away from the process or were downright hostile about it.

Why had this department's collaborative efforts failed to gel when the math department, which had used the same collaborative model, was now a thriving team? Both departments were struggling with large classes and increasingly diverse student populations. Both departments had the same resources and the same number of staff. But as the new department head investigated the problem further, she discovered a number of *contextual* factors that distinguished the two areas:

- The math department staff was considerably younger than her own people and perhaps more open to change.
- Some teachers in the social studies department were still trying to adapt to major curriculum changes that had been brought in two years ago.
- The non-supporters in her own department appeared to gather around a ringleader of sorts. This individual had personality conflicts with the former department head and had never bought into the collaborative efforts. Also he was (or at least she so believed) a bit of a good old boy who did not quite take her leadership seriously.
- Staff felt burdened by the marking requirements in their subject area and noted that social studies and English language arts posed greater

problems for senior high students with weak English language skills.

To begin to address the problem in her area, this social studies department head needed to ask questions, think carefully, and identify factors like those above that made her own department's challenge of implementing collaborative practices distinct from that of the math department. Each department, though provided with the same resources and situated within the same larger context of the school, operated within unique contexts shaped by the demands of differing subject areas, and the histories and personalities of the staff involved.

## Conclusion

To new or non-researchers, research may seem difficult, esoteric, and confusing. The best researchers do things as straightforwardly as possible. Think as simply as possible: if you want to know the answer to a question, ask the question.

Doing research well does not take genius, but it does take care and thoughtful consideration. Qualitative "designs" similar to the ones we have been discussing do not rely on complex methodologies and inferential statistics to extract meaning from research. However, qualitative research decisions are practical and ethical; they stress common sense, consideration for others, and attention to detail.

The methods we have suggested here for defining a problem are fairly generic, but hopefully they illustrate some possible ways to approach your site-based research question and give you a good understanding of how your project should progress. Although you are bound by time because you must graduate, action research is, in many contexts, unbounded. Action research is not usually restrictive in its timeframe; the time needed at various stages depends upon the questions that guide the study and upon the number of co-researchers and participants involved. However, any good action research project always includes the stages of negotiation, reflection, and implementation—sometimes in no particular order. The purpose, as stated often, is to address a problem or question in a workable manner.

## Fig. 4.3 Planning Your Project:
## Key Questions to Consider as You Begin Your Study

### What am I going to research? What are my research questions?
- What is my central question?
- What subquestions must I ask and answer to answer my central question?

### What will my research stance be?
- Do I want to be clinical (to understand and help the client)?
- Am I curious (do I want to find information, truth, or fact)?
- Do I want to make changes to a practice or within an institution?
- What research orientation do I ascribe to?
- What is the overall function of my research?

### To whom do I report?
- For whom am I working?
- Where do I—as a researcher—enter the equation?

### What will I consider as data?
- Where do my data come from?
- What will my data look like?
- How can I organize these data well?

### What research methodologies will I use?
- What method fits my research question?
- How will I collect data?
- What is feasible given time, monetary and logistical constraints?
- In what order should I undertake my research study?
- How can I work effectively and efficiently?
- How can I work ethically?

### How will I evaluate my own research?
- How do I, as a researcher, impact the research?
- How will I know if my data are accurate?
- How will I know if my data are useful?
- What ethical considerations must I attend to?
- What is my relationship to the research and those I involve in my research?
- How have I intruded on the lives of others? (Have I been as psychologically and physically neat and as considerate as possible?)

# FIVE

# *How to Write*
## A LITERATURE REVIEW

*You'll be over your head before you know it,*
*with too much information.*

**IF YOU REALLY CARE ABOUT YOUR RESEARCH,** you will want to talk to others about it. In many ways, doing a literature review is like having a conversation with people who care about the same things you do. The authors of the relevant literature have chosen to invest their time and energies in the same area that you are investigating now. As a result, you will already have much in common. If you *curious)*

think about a literature review as socializing with people who share similar interests, the review takes on an entirely different sense.

Sadly, many graduate researchers see the literature review as a chore—something that must be done before they can begin to work. They do their review, but they do it dutifully rather than with a celebratory or adventurous spirit. This lack of enthusiasm is unfortunate; such researchers miss out on all of the encouragement and advice of others in the academic community about the two most important things in their research project: its content and its methodology.

*— to gain background info – what has been looked at before – other findings*

## Reviewing Literature for Content and Methods

In the olden days of quantitative research, most graduate researchers did a content literature review. Because the methodology of quantitative research was generally taken for granted, there was no need to look at other researchers' designs and methodologies. Today's research world is vastly different. Almost every graduate research thesis has two reviews of literature: one that explicates the content and topic of the research, and another that describes and justifies the methodology to be used by that researcher as he works. Therefore when you read other studies, look for insights both into what has been discovered (the content) and how it has been found and articulated (the methodology). Both of these areas will aid you in your own site-based research project.

### Getting Started

Many research books will tell you that after you have chosen and settled on your research question, the next important step is to learn more about the topic by conducting a research (literature) review. This view is simply not reflective of how real researchers work. Real researchers are never *not* working on their review of literature! Their lives and their work meld together, and they are always reading in the areas of their interests. The two processes of refining a question and reviewing the literature happen at once, much like the site-based research process you've already read about in the previous chapter.

What we are saying is that you only need a germ of an idea to begin working on your literature review. In fact, if your idea is too concrete—if you are stuck in it—you are not open to what you read. You cannot let the literature speak with you or to you. Conversely, if you stay loose and flexible about your own idea(s) and approach the literature with an open mind, it actually helps shape your thinking and your work. Basically, it is never too early to begin your literature review—a sort of mucking around in the primordial goo of research, letting it spring to life where it may. In the step-by-step process that follows in the next section, this sense of natural development is implicit in the process. If you do this right, your work here will be a crucial addition to your project.

## *Reflecting on Your Research With Others*

When you have completed any step of your work, there is no reason not to share your work with those researchers whose work you have consulted, given these days of easy, instant access to others through email. One of Jim's students took the challenge and sent her work to well-known media and culture critic Neil Postman. Not only did Postman respond personally to her ideas, he encouraged her to visit him and talk more!

Your literature review will allow you to gain a better understanding of the topic you have chosen. In all likelihood, it will also begin to reveal some possible solutions to your own organizational dilemma. And that's the deal. This process of conversing with the literature enables a researcher to draw on and share existing knowledge and expertise in her area of interest. Literature reviews are a collaboration of perspectives, and it is important that you take yourself seriously in this collaboration; your thoughts and observations are a valuable contribution to the research community.

## *Synthesizing What You Read*

A literature review is more than a compilation of findings. It is an evaluation of what other scholars and researchers have written about your topic. The literature review is based entirely on the problem or issue that you wish to address and the way in which you will address it. Take ownership of what you learn. To do this work well, you must learn to recognize relevant information, synthesize it, and evaluate its worth for your study.

For example, did you notice a few paragraphs back when we were talking about what most research books tell you about doing a literature review? We *criticized* the notion of beginning your review after choosing your question as failing to understand or communicate how real researchers work. What gives us the right to be so critical about these books? Well, we've put in our time; when you do and teach research as a vocation, you soon learn the work and develop confident stances of your own. You will develop the same confidence and fluency in your own area of interest as you gain experience by consulting and wrestling with the literature.

In short, a good literature review requires:

- **information seeking** – the ability to efficiently scan the literature using manual or computerized search methods to identify a potentially useful selection of articles and books
- **critical appraisal** – the ability to apply principles of analysis to identify those studies that are fair and balanced
- **organized presentation** – the ability to organize literature into meaningful constructs.

– ADAPTED FROM TAYLOR 2001

**Fig. 5.1. Reading Literature Critically**

**While reading the literature, consider the following questions:**

- What crucial issues are noted in the literature?
- What past findings have a bearing on your setting?
- How does your perspective differ from those you have read? How does it agree?
- What has been neglected in the literature?

– BOGDAN AND BIKLEN 1998

When you have completed your work, the information you have organized in your literature must be carefully and systematically recorded, both for your study and for those who follow. Because others will read and consider your work, document the information carefully. Your review of the literature is important because:

- It creates a permanent record for future reference.
- It helps build continuity for the project if the participants change.
- It is a valuable part of sharing your work with others.
- It can be used to support further research, including yours, and perhaps that of others who use it to support applications for funding.

– ACTION RESEARCH GUIDE FOR ALBERTA TEACHERS 2000

## Reading Literature Critically

In 1996, physicist Alan Sokal undertook what he called "a modest (though admittedly uncontrolled) experiment."

He wondered if a leading North American journal of cultural studies would publish a nonsense article if it sounded good and it flattered the editors' preconceptions. This is how his experiment played out. Sokal's article was submitted to the prestigious academic journal *Social Text*, and though his work "Transgressing the Boundaries: Toward a Transformative Hermeneutics of Quantum Gravity" was utterly fabricated and nonsensical, it was published in the journal's Spring/Summer 1996 edition. Simultaneously, Sokal fessed up to his prank in another journal. The result was a good laugh for those who tended to believe— as we do—that published work can tend towards the aggressively esoteric. And his success produced some egg on the face of the folks at *Social Text*. The rest of the academic world was in somewhat of an uproar, but only some of it involved laughter.

While Sokal's actions were perhaps ethically questionable, his point was to challenge what he felt was substandard—yet widely read and published—academic work. His defenders compared him to the child in *The Emperor's New Clothes*, the one who dared to point out the obvious, to use his common sense.

Our purpose in relating this lurid little tale, then, is to encourage you to use your own common sense when something you read strikes you as "off the mark." Certainly we do not suggest that the authenticity of all academic work be loudly challenged; generally, academic work is genuine and serious, and produced by people whose goals are similar to our own. This work is completed (and reviewed by others) carefully and responsibly. However, writers and reviewers have their own perspectives, their own judgments, their own blind spots. We have called these *biases* throughout our book. Whatever you call them, everyone comes to the table with a favourite food.

This leaves you as a neophyte researcher with a little problem. How do you tell the diamond from the rough? The silk purse from the sow's ear? Your challenge is to find good literature that will help you to make decisions and get a sense of where things are in the area you have chosen to understand. Your first task, then, when you do your reading for your literature review is to spot "where your authors are coming from" by using your critical thinking skills along with your own common sense.

Of course you know that a critical read involves much more than simply pronouncing a written work good or bad. As University of Alberta academic researcher Tara Fenwick describes:

> The point is not to tear apart the literature...but to locate a particular text as offering only one perspective (of many) that is:
>
> - partial (there are two—or more—sides to every story);
> - positioned in a distinct way in a particular community;
> - invested with particular desires and assumptions (on the part of the author[s]); and
> - situated in a particular cultural time and place.
>
> – Fenwick and Parsons 2002

Your job, when reading, is (1) to determine what perspective, what "story" is offered by a particular work, and (2) to consider how it applies to your own research project. We hope that providing the following ideas to consider will help you along in this process.

**Considering context.** First, what is the context of the article? By this we mean, where did the article come from and why was it written? Much as newspapers are usually known to be left or right in their political tone, the articles you read can be shaped—or expected to carry certain ideological "markings" depending on their source. For example, in their own ways, journals have a constituency. Some are written for business human resources staff; some are written by and for psychologists; some are written for Marxists; some are written for Oprah fans. When you read, it is wise to know where the author is coming from and where he or she is going. For instance, from the few examples above, how do you think the viewpoints of a Marxist would translate for a typical CEO of a Fortune 500 company in the United States? And these are not the only mixes and matches you might find.

We can also think of differences in *historical* context. For example, we have been working in partnership with another university on a Canadian-based broadband cable study. For whatever reason, to make their work easier or in an attempt to rely upon already established external validity measures, this university has insisted upon using a four-year-old survey instrument that was piloted and normed in the southern United States. Does your critical reading of this situation get your antennae twitching as it does our own? First, the United States—especially the southern states—differs radically from Canada, especially in terms of race, social structure, and education. Second, broadband technology is dynamic and very new, to say the least. Four years is an epoch in such a fast-paced field of study as technology. Our critical reading suggests that the findings of such an enterprise might be suspicious.

The point is to understand that work can get dated—or perhaps not? While most of your reading will probably be quite current, you might want to actually consider older works with some sensitivity to the thoughts and ideas that were current for the time that the article was written. For instance, you've no doubt encountered those ubiquitous terms *life-long learning* and *learning organization*. These terms tend to centre learning in our work environments, where its primary objective is to advance organizations and individual careers. However, if you were to study articles from the 1960s and the 1970s that pertain to adult continuing education, you would find instead a left-to-radical conception of learning. Specifically, adult education was often conceived as a democratic undertaking that would help ordinary people use knowledge to challenge social injustices.

Finally, it is important to consider which organization(s) might be affiliated with the work you are reading. Who does the author "work for"? Who sponsored the research you are reading? One teacher we know recently responded to a government publication on a project she was working on, musing that "They sure dress it up, don't they?" The government branch, of course, had invested a great deal of money in the project, so it had an interest in presenting the work as positively as possible to the public. At the same time, this rather slanted publication also pointed out the structural inequities of the project—she was working for a school district with an obvious lack of funding.

**To persuade or to inform?** Say Laura and Jim are having a typical conversation. Jim asks Laura what she did that morning. Laura says: "I worked on our book this morning and made revisions to Chapters 7 and 8. I had a shower. I drank fourteen cups of coffee." This is a simple exchange of information. It answers questions like Jim's ("What did you do this morning?") as well as other simple questions such as:

- What happened?
- What is going on?
- What is being done here?
- What is being said here?

This is simple stuff—the part that most students find easiest to identify when they read. It is "just the facts, ma'am." (In academic-speak, we ask, "What is the main idea or *thesis* of this work?")

But because we are dealing with qualitative research and because most site-based research projects deal with human behaviour (what we would loosely term the social sciences), you aren't going to encounter too many simple exchanges of facts and information. Remember that we human beings are as quirky and diverse as can be—there are no hard and fast rules about the ways in which we should organize ourselves and interact with one another.

So you won't find too many straight presentations of fact in texts and research. Rather, most of what you read will be an attempt to *persuade* you to agree with the author's beliefs on a given topic. Your job as a critical reader is to look beyond what the person is saying—beyond his or her thesis—to ask the more difficult questions of whether what is being said is reasonable and convincing, and what the arguments presented mean for your research project.

Entire volumes are written about the art and science of critical thinking, and we can hardly do the topic justice in such a short space. Perhaps we can simply raise your awareness of those occasions when you might be reading with *uncritical* acceptance (we all do sometimes) and ask that you interrupt this process with a few simple questions:

- What argument is being presented?
- What persuasive techniques is the author using to encourage you to buy in to her argument? Really, how impressive is the argument presented?
- Are these techniques fair play? Can you conclude that the argument is fair and reasonable? Is it clear that the author understands the argument?
- Finally, how does this argument apply to your work?

Let us give you a quick example of how one might be critical—yet not dismissive—of a piece of academic writing. Peter Vaill (1996) has written what is considered, in some circles, quite a classic book. To be accurate, he makes some excellent points about the nature of organizational life. We say this because we don't want you to believe we are simply dumping on his ideas. However, Vaill seems to use the phrase "permanent white water" (p. 4) in an almost uncritical way. More to the point, some graduate students we have worked with seem to trot out this phrase (notice our use of italics to describe this—that is a hint) to note their general acceptance of a condition they believe exists and that explains the nature of life within organizations. They then leave it as "the truth" as if it had been delivered by the Easter Bunny.

But let us critically consider this language for a minute. First, we really don't think that organizational life is "permanent white water"; the phrase is more "cutsie" than an accurate reflection of the complexities of organizational life. For example, we honestly believe some aspects of organizational culture do *not* change, nor should they. We believe that good relationships always make a better working space. We believe that honest concern for others—even clients—is persuasive. We believe that an organization—even a graduate university—that offers a good product does better than one that is slick but lacks substance. And so on. Second, if we did believe that life was permanent whitewater, what are the implications of holding this belief? Should we lose hope because changes cannot be made? Is there no rock to build one's organizational home upon? Are we driven to a state of permanent ennui because we cannot deal with the ramifications of such a state of turmoil and confusion?

The point is, when you think about this phrase—guess what? There are just times when it doesn't work. Therefore, although we believe Vaill offers insights, we cannot accept everything he says as completely true.

## Fig. 5.2. Persuasive Techniques

### The Art of Persuasion

If you think persuasion is a new concept, you may be surprised to hear that the Greeks—because they were so interested in language—systematically studied the "art" of persuasion many years ago. In fact, the ever-laborious Aristotle categorized persuasion into three distinct types:

*Ethical persuasion (ethos).*
A fundamental persuasive technique that links the persuasive goal to an ethic so powerful or unquestioned that one would hardly think to challenge the claim. This style of persuasion often rests on the credibility of the issue or the presenter. For example, in the case of a credible issue: third world foster child campaigns tap into our belief that children should not starve; in the case of a credible presenter: Bill Cosby likes Jell-O pudding, so you should too.

*Pathetic persuasion (pathos).*
The persuasion technique here is to link the persuasive goal to an emotionally attractive outcome that is so good for you that you would scarce not follow the directives. This is found in the things our fathers would tell us when they said, "Once you get your education, the world will open up before you." It also applies in the case of the spam email that suggests that a certain diet will help you lose 40 pounds in three days.

*Logical persuasion (logos).*
In this case, the fundamental persuasive technique links the persuasive goal to an "understanding" so ingrained in society or a culture that the persuasive goal is hard to resist. We are persuaded when the theory makes sense and is therefore inarguable. This is the sort of thing a company that sells vacuum cleaners might use when they tell you that their product has the newest and most up-to-date features money can buy. Societal logic implies that having the newest and best is what's good for you.

Literature, although much deeper and more educational than most advertisements, must be carefully considered before one buys into it. We must always ask: "What are they selling and how are they selling it?"

## Privileged Views and Voices

Do you remember the story of the seven blind men and the elephant? Each encounters only one part of the elephant—a leg, the trunk, an ear, what have you—so each has a very different idea of what an elephant is like. The "research elephant," of course, is like the truth, and we are all somewhat blind in that we cannot perceive that whole truth; we need the voices and perspectives of others.

There are two implications here. The first is acknowledging your own blind spots. No doubt you bring some of your own ideas and beliefs to the table when you begin your reading. For some the temptation is to read and seriously consider only what *confirms* existing biases. Don't we all want to be right and have a bunch of people agree with us? Unfortunately, this approach can just leave you really right about only one part of the elephant, with a weak understanding of the big picture. In short, read widely and read carefully—and thoughtfully consider what you *don't* agree with, too.

The second implication is that the authors you read are in exactly the same boat. They too have their biases; they too make choices about whether they will explore (or openly reveal) those biases in their work. In other words, a given author may not be seeing the whole elephant either. This is another excellent reason to cast a wide net in your library research. By comparing many works, you develop a stronger sense of where an individual author's biases may lie.

When we speak of "privileging" certain perspectives, we mean that any work—including your own—may be critically examined for the views, beliefs, or groups of people whose interests receive the most attention. Our work as researchers is not about giving special treatment or even compensatory treatment to the subjects of our research. (However, as you will read in this book, we believe all research has a political agenda.)

## Somewhere Between Blind Acceptance and Paranoia...

In student research, we've seen extremes of both blind acceptance and paranoia. Some students take most everything they read as gospel—often because they feel they lack the expertise to challenge what they read. (This, by the way, is not true. If you do not have the expertise to be critical of what you read, drop the desire to gain an advanced degree right now!) Others get so darn carried away with their Critical Thinking Superpowers that they criticize (rather than critique) everything they read and look for hidden agendas and biases everywhere. But most of us muddle about somewhere in the middle, trying to remain open to the ideas we encounter while developing the confidence to challenge and question these ideas when some aspect of them doesn't sit right. It is a careful balance, but one that you will achieve by reading widely and sharing your own thoughts, ideas and responses with critical friends.

### Fig. 5.3. Questions for Critical Reading

The following questions may help you to carefully consider what you read, and to use your own experience, common sense, and critical thinking skills to assess the merit of what your author has to say. Remember, not all academic literature is created equally!

*Purpose*
- Why was this text written?
- What purpose(s) do you think it serves?
- What audience is addressed?

*Historical Context*
- When was the article written?
- Does it reflect the thinking or trends of a given era?

*Authorship*
- Who is the author and what bias(es) or particular perspectives might he bring to the work?
- If these things are stated or evident, how might the author's occupation, politics, or other affiliations shape his thinking?

*Arguments*
- If the author takes a strong position on a topic, how does she represent others?
- Are contrary perspectives addressed? Are they addressed fairly?
- Are issues pertaining to race, class and/or gender fairly portrayed?
- Does the author show sensitivity to different worldviews?

## How to Conduct a Literature Review

This section has two purposes. First, we want to help you look for research literature that you might add to your already partially completed review for your research study. Second, even if you do not know the specific study you will do, be confident that you can begin your review immediately—for in doing the review, you will find the path you need. Frankly, it would be hard for us to imagine that anyone reading this paragraph would not have some idea of the area of research that interests him. It is time to start looking around generally and trusting that your "conversations" with the readings will guide you towards specificity.

If you are like other graduate students, you have chosen a topic but have not quite decided how you will conduct your research—that is, you have not decided what your research methods will be. Very soon, you will need to choose a methodology. However, even if you have not made this decision, we believe you should begin to work on your literature review anyway. We trust that this activity will help you to decide what research methods you will use as you answer your research questions.

*Think of a literature review as socializing with people
who share similar interests.*

We know that you know the area of your study. Your task now is to use what you already know to seek information about what other researchers have found. Remember that these researchers already care about the same problems you do and have already done their work. You will use what they have learned to further your own understanding.

Remember that a review of literature should be fun—a community celebration sort of like Christmas morning. Relax and enjoy. We encourage you not to miss possibilities; read thoroughly and don't rush! In fact, reading thoroughly in the first place actually saves you time in the long run. Some of the work you read may not directly transfer into your final research project; however, the process of reviewing the literature and the information you discover will help you to complete your own study. Why repeat what someone else has already done?

Remember as you read the research literature to keep notes in a way that best suits your own note-taking style.

## Doing Your Research

Recall from earlier sections that you are actually working on two research goals: (1) to discover literature that addresses your own research study, and (2) to help you decide what research methodology to use. For this activity, it doesn't matter which goal you are pursuing. All roads lead to Rome, as they say. As practising researchers, these are the methods we use to complete our work. Generally speaking, you will:

1. Conduct a search on the internet using key terms
2. Generate a collection of twenty-five to thirty articles to use for your literature review
3. Read these articles and taking notes
4. Organize your notes into an outline
5. Use the outline to write your literature review.

As best as possible, we've tried to break this lengthy process into a series of steps that have worked well for us in the past. Don't become overwhelmed as you read through this the first time. It seems like a lot at first, but if you follow the steps one at a time, everything will become clear.

**Step 1: Make a map.** If you have a general idea of the research methods you want to use, begin by making a point-form outline or a concept map of what you already know. We love to start with concept maps or mind maps because they don't push the information too quickly; they're kind of a mental warm-up. If you are able to complete this task easily, jump right to Step 3. If this task was difficult and you're still confused about the specifics of what you want to research, go to Step 2. In either case, don't worry—you can get there from here!

**Step 2: Start to work.** If you are still deciding what (specifically) you want to research or you haven't decided what research method you will use, there is still no reason for concern. It doesn't mean that you can't—or shouldn't—start working. It just means that you will be looking at both content and methodologies in your review. Just choose the initial (or general) methods that interest you. You will naturally narrow your focus as you read more.

**Step 3: Organize in advance.** If you are now fairly clear on your topic and methodology, the next step is to make space to collect your information. Use a floppy disk, CD, or similar, or create a folder on your hard drive. Because you will be using the internet for this portion of your work, get in the habit of saving your work as you go. It could potentially save you a lot of time and grief later! If you use the internet, this may mean creating word files complete with http addresses and the dates you accessed each site.

**Step 4: Visit the library.** If you are confused about where to search, visit your university library's website, which provides a number of online resources to help you. Better yet, if you can, go right into the library and talk to a real flesh-and-blood librarian (they still exist). Resource desks are there to help you. Work with your librarians! These people are the Angels of the Archives; they know their stuff and they want to help.

**Step 5: Determine your keywords.** When you have figured out which data-bases to search, decide what keywords to use in the search. This is where your mind map or concept map can be helpful. Notice the words you used to describe the area or topic of your study, and begin searching with these words as your key terms. Don't be discouraged if at first they don't work. You will need to play around and explore, as the English language is filled with synonyms. You may be onto something wonderful, but perhaps have not yet been initiated into the language of the topic.

**Step 6: Be selective.** Once you've found keywords that work, choose about twenty-five of the best and most relevant articles. Save these on your hard drive, and limit yourself to working through these before doing any more searches. Some people go crazy and begin to review everything, but don't be seduced or you'll be in over your head before you know it, with too much information. Review only the number of articles you picked at the start.

**Step 7: Read in brief.** Scan the articles or read the abstracts to get the lay of the land. You are probably anxious to read, or you may see greater value in just diving into the whole text. However, from our experience, abstracts are valuable tools. They can save you lots of time in these early stages, where your goal is to get a general feel for the area you are researching. Save your thorough reading for a little later in this process.

**Step 8: Build your references.** As you save and review your articles, take the time to copy complete references. Get in the habit of keeping good consistent bibliographical references from the start. This will save you tons of time and aggravation in the long run.

## *Reading and Taking Notes on the Computer*

Once you've skimmed over your articles, it is time to read more thoroughly and take notes. The method we outline below assumes you are reading and taking notes on the computer as you go. If you are a "print person" and prefer to work with hard copies of the literature, jump straight down to the next section, "Reading and Taking Notes on Paper," which gives instructions for reading and note taking the old-fashioned way. "Computer people," read on.

1.  Open two documents on your computer. Name the first BIBLIOGRAPHY and the second NOTES.

2.  Now open the first article you've saved. Because this is the first article you will read, we are going to call this ARTICLE 1. Rename the document with the number 1 at the front. For example, the article "Organizational Theory.doc" would become "1 Organizational Theory.doc." Save under the new name.

3.  Copy the article's full citation, and paste one copy in your BIBLIOGRAPHY and one copy in your NOTES. Include the article number (1) with each citation. You have now created a cross-referencing system that will keep the article, its citation, and your notes on the article linked with one reference number.

4.  In your NOTES document underneath the citation you've copied, begin to take notes on the first article as you read thoroughly. Cut and paste any direct quotes from the article that you feel may be helpful. Be sure to record the page numbers as you do so.

5.  Repeat the process with the second article you open and read, renaming it as ARTICLE 2 and copying its citation to your BIBLIOGRAPHY and NOTES. Take your notes for the second article underneath its citation in your NOTES document.

*Very helpful*

6.  Continue this process with each of the articles you read. Be sure that the article number and citation number match. When you are finished, you should have a BIBLIOGRAPHY that contains each of your numbered articles' citations in the order you've read them and a fairly lengthy NOTES document that contains the citation and your notes for each article, again in the order you've read them.

**Fig. 5.4. Document layout for taking notes on computer.**

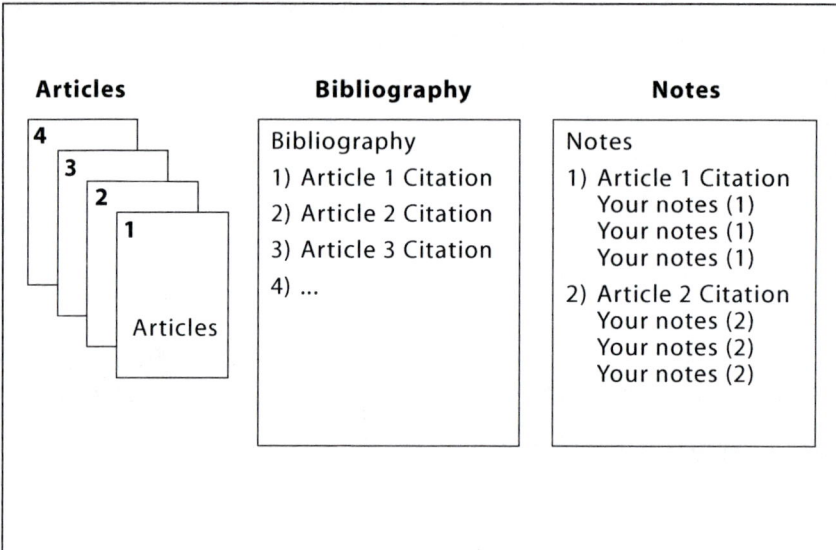

7.  Now turn your attention to the NOTES document you have created. Read your notes over on the screen. As you read, do the following:

-   Add any brief personal comments or observations right into the text as you go. We say "brief" because we are still taking notes; we don't want you to start writing just yet, but we don't want you to miss any ideas either.
-   When you have completed your reading, write a short phrase—just a few words—that summarizes what each note is about. Try to

categorize your notes using a set number of summary phrases (we recommend somewhere in the neighbourhood of four to seven topic headings). These categories will help you to sort the notes into usable themes or subsections for your literature review. If you don't know what to call a particular note, create a "Miscellaneous" category for now.

- At the beginning of each of your notes, type the number of the article/citation to which it corresponds.

8. Now, open a new document in your computer called SORTED NOTES. List the category phrases (headings) that you used to identify your notes in the last step. These will serve as a rough outline for your literature review. Don't sweat the organization of these categories too much right now. This is not *The Old Man and the Sea*; a literature review is not a novel! Just choose an order for your categories and stick with it. The sections of the final document are easily moved around in entire blocks anyway, if you change your mind later.

9. Copy the first note in your NOTES document and paste it into its correct category in SORTED NOTES.

10. Repeat this process with each of your notes. When you are finished, you will have sorted all your notes by the categories you've ascribed to them.

11. Print the document SORTED NOTES.

12. The next step is to literally cut and paste the notes in each category into an order that seems logical—again remembering that the final order can be almost any logical structure. Working with one category or theme at a time, cut out your printed notes and use a glue stick to paste them in the correct (logical) order on another sheet of paper. Do the same for each category until the task is completed.

13. Return to your computer and reorganize each section of SORTED NOTES on your screen by moving the notes into the order that you cut-and-pasted them into in the last step. (Remember not to lose the article reference numbers as you work.) You have now created the first draft of your literature review.

14. Now you can begin to write, editing the notes into a smooth, readable format. Replace the article numbers in your notes with proper references

to the articles. Link the sections together with appropriate transitions. Remember that you will go through three or four quick revisions, so don't try to make all the changes the first time through. Just read and edit what gets your attention as you go. Add your own thoughts, evaluations, and critiques as you write and revise.

15. When you've done a number of revisions, you are ready to write a one- or two-paragraph introduction section and a one- or two-paragraph conclusion. These can say whatever you want, but an introduction usually sets out the themes or titles to follow, lists the areas or types of journals (like "Business" or "Medicine") where you found the best literature, and gives the reader a clue about what's coming. The conclusion basically summarizes the literature review and pulls three or four highlights from it. It also introduces the next section of the study, which is usually the methodology.

16. Save your BIBLIOGRAPHY. Remove the reference numbers and sort your citations alphabetically. Be sure to review the bibliography for conformity to APA standards.

17. Congratulations! You're done the literature review section of your project final report.

## Reading and Taking Notes on Paper

If you prefer to take notes on computer as we've described above, skip right over this section and go to "What Does the Finished Literature Review Look Like?" in the section below. If you are a print person who processes things better via the good old-fashioned written page or who would rather read in bed or at your favourite coffee hangout than be glued to a computer screen, read on. You will start your note-taking process with the stack of articles you have printed off to read.

1. First, you may want to photocopy your articles. Later, you'll be messing them up with highlighters, notes, and scissors. You may want a "clean" copy of the articles in print form to refer back to later.

2. Call the first article you read ARTICLE 1. (Write this in large letters right on the first page.)

3. Name a blank sheet of paper CATEGORIES.

4. Begin reading your first article. When you come across something note-worthy, you'll need to:

   - Highlight it.
   - Write the article number in the margin beside the section you've highlighted, and also in the margin write a one- or two-word category that your note would fit into.
   - List each category on the CATEGORIES sheet.

5. As you highlight new notes, either assign them to an existing category or create new categories as needed, adding each new category to your CATEGORIES sheet. Later, you'll be using these categories to organize your literature review into sections, so keep this in mind as you choose them. Ideally, you should have between four and seven categories to work from.

6. Name a separate sheet of paper PERSONAL IDEAS. As you read, record any thoughts or ideas that come to you. Be sure to label each note you make here with (a) the article number it pertains to, and (b) the category it would fit into.

7. Repeat this process with each article you read, numbering the articles as you go.

8. When you have finished reading and highlighting all of your articles, turn your attention to the CATEGORIES sheet you created. Can you picture how these categories might be used to organize your literature review? Do you need to combine some categories to make the process more manageable? In what order do they make the most sense for now?

9. Now you will need a handful of large (preferably used or recycled) envelopes. Label the front of each envelope with a category. Label one additional envelope CITATIONS.

10. Return to the pile of articles you have read and highlighted. Cut out the sections you highlighted, making sure that each includes your margin notes of (1) the article number the section comes from, and (2) the category it fits into. As you cut, stuff each section into its corresponding category envelope. For each article, you should also cut out the citation and stuff it in the CITATIONS envelope. Once you have finished cutting out the good stuff, the rest of your scraps can be tossed out.

11. You will need some workspace for the next step, plus a glue stick and some paper (you can use recycled paper for this; you only need one "good" side to work on). Take the first envelope and dump your cuttings on the table. Look them over, then glue them onto the paper in some order that makes sense to you. Remember that there are many right answers when it comes to ordering the information—writing a review of literature is not like writing a poem. The point is, don't sweat this too much. You can make changes later if you feel the need to. Remember to number the sheets so you can review them in the correct order. Return the sheets you have glued together back to the envelope.

12. Repeat this process with each of the envelopes and categories.

13. Turn to your CITATIONS envelope. Glue the individual citations onto a piece of paper in numeric order; that is, the order in which you initially read the articles. You will use this sheet to help you write the draft of your literature review. Here is what you should have in front of you by now:

**Fig. 5.5. Document layout for taking notes on paper.**

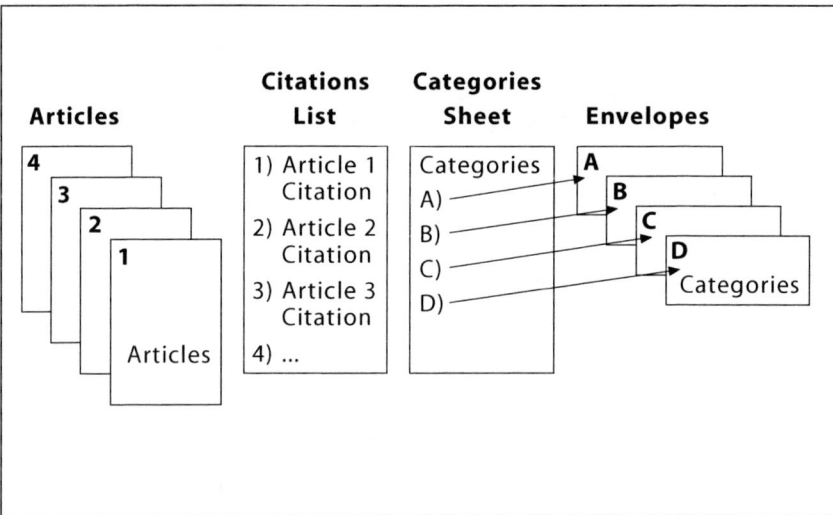

14. Now you are ready to convert your notes into a readable format. It is important right now that you don't try to do too much—remember, one step at a time! Key your cut-and-paste notes into the computer. Referring to your CITATIONS sheet, replace numbers in the notes with proper references. You may add any other notes as they come to you, but don't let this slow you down. Work as quickly as possible and don't worry too much about editing right now—you can do this later. One thing at a time!

15. Now you can begin to write, editing the notes into a smooth, readable format. Link the sections together with appropriate transitions. Remember that you will go through three or four quick revisions, so don't try to make all the changes the first time through. Just read and edit what gets your attention as you go. Refer to your sheet of PERSONAL IDEAS to add your own thoughts, evaluations, and critiques as you write and revise.

16. When you've done a number of revisions, you are ready to write a one- or two-paragraph introduction section and a one- or two-paragraph conclusion. These can say whatever you want, but an introduction usually sets out the themes or titles to follow, lists the areas or types of journals (like "Business" or "Medical") where you found the best literature, and gives the reader a clue about what's coming. The conclusion basically summarizes the literature review and pulls three or four highlights from it. It also introduces the next section of the study, which is usually the methodology.

17. Use your cut-and-paste page of CITATIONS to write your bibliography. Be sure to review the bibliography for conformity to APA standards.

18. Congratulations! You're done the literature review section of your project.

# What Does the Finished Literature Review Look Like?

For those new to writing literature reviews, the paragraph below offers a model for writing. Note that the author and the year usually come first in the sentence, followed by what the author(s) found. Consult an appropriate style guide for some more advice on including references in your text. Most social sciences use APA (American Psychological Association) formatting. You can buy the book (now in its fifth edition), but you may very well be able to get by on the many, many "unofficial" style guides online. Use the keywords "APA style" in your search engine to locate these.

As you write, don't worry too much about the verbs used to report the authors' statements—verbs like Brown *said* or Smith *reported*, and so on—but do try to write with some literacy. Don't repeat the same verb over and over again: *said, said, said*. Finally, if you can offer some critical commentary, do so. Try to engage the work and mould it to the needs of your own research rather than just listing off what you've found like so many numbers in a phone book. Writing a literature review is much like repeating a group discussion that you had with several people, and it can be written as such.

**Fig. 5.6.**

**Jim and Laura's Lit Review Verbs: You Too Can Write a Lit Review**

Writing literature reviews is downright formulaic once you get the hang of it. It's simply a matter of listing your review findings in a logical fashion and mixing up your verbs a little to make your writing more interesting. Read the example on the next page to see if you can find the verbs listed here...

| | | |
|---|---|---|
| • observes | • warns | • finds |
| • challenges | • challenges | • concurs |
| • states | • agrees | • suggests |
| • says | • explains | • proposes |
| • believes | • reiterates | |
| • cautions | • echoes | |

Here's a sample paragraph for a literature review. We've taken the notes that would have been drafted in the research/reading stage and written them into a polished format. First, the raw notes:

(2) Not appropriate for orgs. that prefer control and predictable outcomes (Bowen 1994)

(7) Weakness of mentoring—leaders need advanced agendas, grasp of potential outcomes or goes nowhere (Meat and Potatoes 1996)

- Better if agenda determined by participants, but they have to be committed
- Mentorship holistic, non-linear

(3) Soup & Sand re: Bowen (1999). Method successful when: clear purpose, high commitment by participants, leaders to work both w. process and its outcomes

(12) Schmuckly re: Bowen. "this technique works best in situations characterized by uncertainty, ambiguity, and a recognition that new ideas are needed." (1994, p. 4)

(6) Sweet and Sour (1996, p. 129). "the participants must volunteer and they will reorganize their marbles based on personal interest and their ability to rub their heads and pat their bellies at the same time."

Ta-da! Now you want to "write through" the raw notes, making sense and keeping it conversational as you go:

Jack Bowen (1994) cautions organizations that prefer control and predictable outcomes not to consider this approach. Meat and Potatoes (1996) believe the weakness of mentoring is the lack of control by leaders who attempt to work without advanced agendas or notions about potential outcomes. Since the agenda is determined by the participants, people must take responsibility, be open, and work in a process that is holistic, not linear. Furthermore, expert facilitation is required. According to Soup and Sandwich (1999), Bowen's method has been most successful when the purpose is clear and there is a high commitment on the part of participants and senior leaders to honour the outcome and process. Schmuckly (1994) observes, through his experience with Bowen's method, that "this technique works best in situations characterized by uncertainty, ambiguity, and a recognition that new ideas are needed." Sweet and Sour (1996) observe that "the participants must volunteer and they will reorganize their marbles based on personal interest and their ability to rub their heads and pat their bellies at the same time."

And you are done!

# SIX

# Designing a Plan of Attack:
## YOUR RESEARCH METHODOLOGY

*To some extent, your biases always shape what you see.*

**THERE'S TALK AND THERE'S ACTION.** Once you have figured out what research you want to do, the next step is figuring out how you will do that research. If you have done your work well, you have set the table by making decisions that stem from your interests (including the needs of the organization for whom you are working) and by reading what others have done who are also interested in this area. This background research and your literature review are, more or less, in the bag, and you are ready to develop a plan that suits your research. Now you must design the process of creating a workable proposal for your research project.

The point of a research plan is to:

- provide an organized (we think it should be step-by-step) structure that will help you conduct your research project and collect the data you need to report, and
- provide those who read your work with insight into what you have done to get to your project's destination.

One of the attractive features of site-based research is that it is more a philosophy than a hard and fast strategy. This means that it can be completed using a wide variety of appropriate methods. Just as the definition of the problem or challenge is negotiated between the researcher and the researched, methodology can be negotiated as well. Your specific methods will be chosen (or constructed) because they have the best chance of actually working—of doing the task the researcher and the participants hope it will do.

In this section, we review (in a very cursory nuts-and-bolts way) the sorts of activities you can use to conduct the actual research within your organization. Perhaps more importantly, we offer some advice about structuring these activities into a workable, step-by-step plan. As so often seems to be the case, effort expended in initial planning saves lots of grief later!

## How to Find Out What You Want to Know

When collecting data about research subjects, there really are only a few ways to go at it. Todd Jick's important and classic research article "Mixing Qualitative and Quantitative Methods: Triangulation in Action" (1979) suggests how very simple collecting data can be. Jick says there are basically only four ways to find out about research subjects.

1.  Ask research participants directly. (Use interviews, questionnaires, and self-reports.)

2. Ask research participants indirectly. (Use psychological instruments or projective tests. Myers-Briggs is one you probably know.)
3. Ask those who interact with the research participants. (Ask co-workers about their observations or perceptions.)
4. Observe the participant's actions or past actions. (Observe and/or analyze the documents, text, or context of the person's situation.)

Of course there are many subcategories, and each strategy itself could be the basis of an entire book on research methodology. Volumes, for example, have been written on observation strategies, from the early anthropology of Margaret Mead to the participant observation studies where the researcher joins in with the activities of the group that he or she is studying. Some great examples of participant observation include Marsh's study of football hooligans (1978) and Corsaro's studies of children's friendships (1985).

However, good research is mostly just good common sense and can be done—and done well—by any careful and attentive researcher. Site-based research projects may use combinations of quantitative and qualitative methods. You may choose any of the techniques we've mentioned already. However, the most typical site-based research projects include interviews, observations, or document analysis. Following is a more detailed explanation of these methods.

**Interviews.** Most research methods are not all that difficult—hardly rocket science. And among all the methodologies, an interview may be the most straightforward research method of any. Basically, the researcher figures out what she wants to know and asks the person whom she believes knows.

For example, one year a graduate student wanted to know how health/wellness consultants worked, so she found and contacted a small number of health/wellness consultants and spoke with them about their work. To gain similar information from these participants, whose common work was the focus of her inquiry, she conducted a "structured interview." This means that she set out a series of specific questions she desired answers to and asked each of the participants the same questions. Her data-collection instrument was a document containing a small number of questions, and she asked each and every interviewee each question in a systematic and precise fashion. Her conversations might have differed, as you would expect from human to human, but she was careful to ask and record answers to each question.

Such a structured interview uses a short instrument to gather data face to face or, sometimes, over the telephone or chat line. Although we have never conducted a computer-based interview, we suspect that it is highly possible. We can also see ways that a data-collection instrument might be stored in a computer and the interviewer might record responses directly onto a computer.

Because interviews take time and require transcription later (although some recent students have had great success with court reporter–type stenographers who provide an immediate transcription at the end of a session, with not much difference in cost), a researcher needs to compare the benefits of different types of interviews or surveys. It might, for example, be easier and cheaper—and result in almost as good responses—to simply mail questionnaires to participants. Researchers must consider the "bang for the buck" ratio—in terms of finances, time, and energy—in choosing one research method over another. As we have often stated, less elegant is generally better than more elegant.

When creating a set of structured interview questions, the researcher must first create a broad set of questions that participants should answer. Second, the researcher should organize broad goals into a smaller, finite number of questions. Often, novice researchers create a huge list of questions, when a few would do just as nicely. They forget one maxim that we believe wholeheartedly: "Every person's favourite topic is himself/herself." This is not a cynical comment, simply a recognition that one question and the ensuing conversation can uncover a whole world of insight.

Interviews are used to allow participants to share their situations and to give each person a voice and opportunity to be heard. Because research must be done ethically, a researcher should always seek permission to ask questions and to record conversations. There is no reason for an interviewer to question or challenge the views of the participant. The point of an interview is to gain the participant's perspective. One major problem with interviews is interviewer bias, which includes not just active bias but also passive bias, such as an inability to consider all the possible questions that could be asked. This is why critical friends are helpful when constructing an interview agenda.

**Observations.** Observations allow the researcher to examine the setting and natural environment of the participants. Remember that context is important. Examining the context involves looking carefully and writing clear, detailed descriptions. Observations are always valuable, but have some drawbacks, such as interrupting or disturbing participants.

One decision that must be made about observation is the degree to which you, the observer, will be interacting with your research subjects. Your involvement will depend on the goals of your observation, the expectations and wishes of your research subjects, and your own familiarity with the research environment. Some examples here may help.

**Example 1.** *A researcher is studying the leadership qualities of a volunteer board's chairperson. He observes a board meeting, but sits quietly in the corner, taking notes, because he wants to see how the chair and board members relate and make decisions at a typical meeting. Here, his involvement might interfere with this goal.*

**Example 2.** *A researcher is evaluating the effectiveness of the services offered at a drop-in centre in a high-needs community. Statistics reveal which programs are used the most or the least, but don't tell her much about how clients view the programs or why they access them. To learn more, the researcher spends several afternoons as a volunteer in various centre programs, observing how they work, and visiting with clients. The process enriches her understanding of the drop-in centre and helps her to build trusting relationships with its clients in preparation for the formal interviews she hopes to conduct later in her study.*

Again, it is less a question of whether your direct involvement (or what is usually called *participant observation*) will influence the actions of your research subjects. Simply put, it will. Rather, ask whether your interaction with the people you are observing will further your research objective or hinder it. As you can see from the examples above, each case will present unique needs and responses.

The important thing for you as a researcher to remember is that, interacting or not, your observations are always shaped to some degree by your own biases. Simple awareness of this fact will help you to represent what you see and hear more fairly. Another possibility is to have another person involved in your project undertake the observations with you, creating a second perspective and set of notes. Follow up by comparing your findings with the other person.

**Document analysis.** As Jim tells it, his initial love for document analysis arose several years ago during a flight from Phoenix to Dallas. (By the way, this was the flight where the attendant told passengers over the plane's intercom that smoking was absolutely prohibited in the plane's restrooms and that anyone caught smoking would be asked to leave the plane immediately. Obviously, a new "get tough" policy.) Anyway, the flight was short and passengers were given a small basket that included a sandwich and a soft drink and some chips. But what was so great about the basket was the little paper doily that separated the food from the basket. The doily was basically a throwaway, but it was beautifully designed. The design was cut paper, perfectly systematic and organized. In fact, the designer had copyrighted the design—his name was on the back with the copyright date.

> Suddenly, I was overcome by what I was seeing. Our culture had honoured creativity by allowing a creator to register the creation. The man had probably sent his mother a copy (if she was alive). The aesthetic of the paper was a system of round and, to my mind, beautiful squiggles and paper pressings, perfectly formed and repeated across the face of the small paper. And this artistic creation was being used for a specific func-tion—and it was temporary. The flight attendant was actually moving up and down the aisle, tossing these beautiful and heart-felt (the man was obviously proud, hence the copyright) creation away.
>
> No one seemed as panicked as I was about this travesty. So I gently put the paper doily into my briefcase, where it stayed for years and was a regular touchstone of my research insight. From this "document," I moved on to analyzing magazine commercials and layouts as cultural artifacts in order to lift out their cultural significance. These days, whenever I teach research document analysis, I ask students to analyze the cultural meanings of Canada embedded in hockey cards.
>
> – Jim

Have you ever noticed that hockey referees wear black-and-white-striped uniforms? Perhaps this is a not-so-obvious reference (note the same root word as referee) to the yin-yang sorts of calls that a hockey ref must make in a game? Is one team good (symbolized in our society by white) and another bad (symbolized by black)? In this same way, a university I have worked with is probably best symbolized by the icon of a castle, which is an interesting juxtaposition with the university's reputation for innovative programming. How might this impact the culture of the institution? That would be a document analysis question—as would be the photos of the learners in the university's handbook or advertising.

Document analysis originated from the idea of hermeneutical learning. **Hermeneutics** is the study of text—and anything from a photo to a story to the layout of a room can be a text. Hermeneutics first began with a study of the Holy Bible, because people wanted to understand what the Bible had to teach modern people. The hermeneutic researcher asks three questions:

1. What does/do the story/text/words mean? (Define the terms.)
2. What did the story/text/words mean to the audience who originally heard it? (In biblical terms, for those who first listened to the parables, for example.)
3. What do these stories/texts/words mean for us today?

These same questions can be asked today with photos, symbols, or cultural artifacts. Take, for example, a Calvin Klein magazine ad. Who is in the ad? Man or woman? Thin or not? Long hair or short? Young or old? What is the ad for? Smelly stuff—if so, why? What does this say about the need to smell good? How is the person clothed, and so what? What does all of this—synthesized—tell us about our culture and society? And this said, what should we do with it?

You can see the possibilities for studies of organizations. How can one's corporate logo or motto be interpreted? Does it really represent the values of the organization? These and many more questions are of the sort that may arise from document analysis.

The point of document analysis is to find significant information embedded in the documents and/or artifacts of the organization you are studying. Insights can be drawn from documents such as memos, minutes, records, official reports, policy statements, procedure statements, plans, evaluation reports, press accounts, public relations materials, information statements, and newsletters. Even the advertisements an organization chooses or the way it arranges and uses its physical space—

including how the CEO shapes her office and what sorts of pictures are on the walls—can tell much about what that organization really values.

It is possible to discover real meanings from stated meanings in this activity, but because there are often huge quantities of documents, this task can be daunting. It is probably wise to scan paper documents briefly for relevant information before committing your time to dealing with them in detail (Stringer 1999).

**Surveys.** Survey research is a method that allows the researcher to acquire data and opinions from a population. This could be an entire population (like the Canadian federal government's census) or a representative sample of a population. Surveys can be a useful tool for both public and private sector organizations and leaders: government, health care providers, universities, private businesses, and others. Because of their versatility, surveys are a meat-and-potatoes-type staple of many research projects.

Surveys can be broad in their scope and content, reaching large groups and gathering large quantities of statistical data with relative speed and ease. For example, researchers may want to discover some part of the public's opinion about graduate programs, political issues or candidates, consumer products, or a variety of other topics. The process is simple, actually: figure out what you want to know and whom you want to ask, then write a series of questions that would elicit the information you need. Once this information is obtained, it can then be used to make decisions, develop new programs, improve service, influence decision makers, and so on. The number of people who want to gain insight about topics is almost endless!

Surveys are used for one simple reason: researchers cannot interview everyone. As a result, they try to find a "representative sample" of the group they want to gain information from or about and then assume that this sample represents the thousands (or sometimes even millions) of people who have similar opinions and preferences. Researchers assume that the opinion of the respondent is similar to the opinion of those people the respondent speaks for. For example, if you want to gain both a general sense of what a group of people think, you might ask a large number of them using a survey instrument. These data can be used to gain insight into trends or relationships, to generally understand attitudes or behaviours, or to make decisions about the next step in a research agenda.

One question on that survey instrument might ask if the participant would like to be involved in an interview that focuses more specifically on the topic in question. In this way, a researcher could gain a smaller group of potential interviewees who would be willing to spend more time explicating the topic. Individual interviews can be used to flesh out the information gained in the broader survey questions.

As with any form of research, researchers must conduct their surveys in an ethical manner. That means that they must respect the participants' right to privacy or non-participation. As a survey researcher you should never divulge the identity of your participants, their personal information, or their specific answers unless you have their permission in writing to do so. A clear and informative cover letter—something we'll discuss in the next chapter— should accompany any survey you use, and it should explain rights and ethical considerations to participants.

Surveys may be simple—for example, we have seen a wonderful five-question survey—but can be complex in their application. They are almost always question-forced answer format, but they can be collected by phone, mail, in person, and increasingly today, over the internet. However the data are collected, the goal of surveys and questionnaires is to collect data from a large number of people.

Some survey methods used in site-based research may be very passive. For example, one graduate student set up a survey on a website used by the sort of participants he wanted to be part of his study. The survey was brief but continued throughout an entire year. This was not his only data-collecting tool, but it added a further triangulated insight into his work.

## Writing Up Your Methods

With any good research, it is important that the researcher obtain data from a wide variety of sources. Such triangulation strengthens the validity of the information obtained. In action research, data are gathered for different purposes at different points in the process. Baseline data determine the extent of a problem (How big is the problem?) and clarifies the existing situation (What is going on?). Research data measure the impact of the intervention (Am I making a difference? Is the situation changing?).

*Triangulation means approaching the problem
from different angles.*

The above questions are crucial, and you need to ask and answer each one when you begin to structure your own research plan. If you are or have been a teacher (and this does not necessarily mean in a school), this part is easy because you are used to writing lesson plans. Writing up your research methods is like writing a detailed lesson plan. If you are not a teacher, perhaps the next best way to think about writing a research method is to think about the directions for putting IKEA furniture together. These directions are specific—sort of match-bolt-C-to-screw-A stuff.

There are always choices about how much specificity to include, and you could approach your study with less specific consideration about these directions. However, you would be wrong to do so. Research should be fun, but, because you are working with participants who must be protected, you are ethically bound to conduct research well. To be slapdash would be simply unethical. Do it right or quit right now!

So how should you begin to write your methods? The answer is to think about all the things—each and every activity—you must do if you are to do the research well, and write them down as a series of specific steps. Then review these steps to see if anything is missing. Next, give the steps (your methods) to a critical friend and ask her to read them. Can she follow the process? Is there a step that is confusing? If so, look at it again. It is tough to think of everything, especially the first time you write research methods. Again, and you have heard it before from us, a critical friend is helpful.

The National Staff Development Council (2000, p. 2) suggests that a researcher should work to corner her question or problem by following this procedure:

- Match data sources to the research question
- Collect data from as many sources as possible
- Keep a data log that includes the date, time, and information collected
- Organize your data around themes, key issues, or topics.

## A Sample Research Plan

The following is an adaptation of a beginning research methodology that was completed by a student before she began her study. Notice the detail and the steps. Things did change, and surprises did happen. That's life. In fact, all research is rife with change and with the need to make quick, by-the-seat-of-your-pants decisions. Still, the point is that she tried to think of everything prior to setting out on the study. Here is her proposed site-based research plan.

1. Compile a community profile of the Greater Edmonton area.
2. Based on information gathered from local organizations, develop a survey, conduct a small number of interviews, and/or hold a focus-group discussion to determine the perceptions of these organizations regarding current and future mentorship challenges facing Edmonton. Consider foreseeable community issues/problems and areas requiring priority attention as perceived by these organizations.
3. Begin to analyze the data gathered from the literature review, the survey, and interviews.

4. Complete the analysis of the gathered data. Write notes about what it might mean for my study.

5. Begin to draft a report of the preliminary findings, together with some general recommendations to have available for an initial meeting of three to four leaders of the YMCA to share at the meeting in late September to early October.

6. Share this draft report with the steering committee of the Edmonton YMCA to receive feedback.

7. Develop a strategy for communicating these preliminary findings at this initial meeting of YMCA leaders in late September to early October.

8. Share relevant data with the various committees that will be developed as part of the organization of the new YMCA (Edmonton) program, in particular the curriculum committee, the leader/trainee selection committee, and the committee responsible for funding.

9. Continue to gather feedback and comments about the findings from the various committees.

10. Be available to meet with the advisory committee that will be established for Edmonton's YMCA to share my research findings.

11. Begin to write the final major project report.

12. Forward the draft of the final report to the project supervisor and the Edmonton YMCA.

13. Make revisions to the draft report based on feedback received.

14. Complete project report.

15. Submit copies of project report to project supervisor for sign-off.

## Collecting Good Data

The central focus of your research plan is to lead you through the collection of data and to do it effectively, efficiently, and ethically. Successful data collection in all research projects is developed around three simple questions:

1. What data are to be collected?
2. How will the data be collected?
3. Who or what sources will provide the data?

The amount of data, or evidence, you gather will depend on how big your research project is. Is your focus confined to a small group of participants? Is your focus an entire organization, like a whole school or business?

When doing any research study, although there will be surprises, it is best to determine which data are (note that the word *data* is plural) most suitable before deciding how and when to collect them. Therefore, a key step in developing your research plan is to examine your alternatives. The choice is one part pragmatic and one part ethical. What should you do? What are the reasonable limits of what you can do?

A good first step is to figure out who knows what. If you can do this, it is easier to list potential sources of data and from whom data could be collected. Then, ask yourself which sources answer your research question and subquestions most directly. Next, prioritize these sources in terms of relevance and importance to your study. Finally, ask yourself if there is anything wrong (unethical) about asking these people to participate. For example, will their participation harm them in some way?

The question of potential harm might be more of a real problem than it first seems. Here's an example, the like of which has happened more than once in a research project. A graduate researcher sees a problem within her organization. In her prospectus, her proposal, and the first chapter of her report she spells out the problem, thus justifying her engagement with it for her project. Her boss—in a higher management position within this organization—reads the work. Frankly, it doesn't sit well. This young upstart is talking about his company—his life—and spelling out the difficulties that will be solved by this research! He is angry and feels blamed. He reads on to see complaint after complaint from those employees who participated—all people he thought were loyal workers in the company.

Can you see where this is going? The reader's bias (in this case, a good thing because he loves the organization) is so strong that the work can never be read without personal engagement. As a researcher, never forget that you are dealing with people's lives and loves. These people, especially if they are good at their work, have invested in it. Therefore, they have vested interests in the research you are doing. That's what makes research worth doing. It is also what makes doing the research a delicate proposition. So do research delicately and with consideration for yourself, your organization, and your participants.

Once you have chosen and prioritized your sources of data, you will have a better idea what data you might gather easily and what data might be more difficult to collect. Eventually your research plan should include a description of the data you will use and how, when, and how often you plan on gathering it.

A final consideration, and one many researchers forget, is how to report your data. Remember that the reporting of research is part of doing research, not something that comes after the research is done. Choose methods that give you data output that already looks like something you can report systematically.

## Planning Tips

Here are some ideas for designing a successful data-collection plan.

**Keep the research manageable.** Start focused and stay focused by identifying your central question and subquestion(s) before starting to gather data. Before deciding to gather new data, seek out and read others' completed research to find out what data exist. Depend on your research "ancestors" and build on their work. Use multiple data sources or research methods. Triangulation helps you locate your central, guiding target.

**Make a plan and stick to it, unless there is very good reason to change.** When planning your research study, consider the following points:

- Planning is a process. Trust the process.
- Make your plan flexible enough to guide your evolving inquiry without stunting its growth. The plan is a map, not the territory.
- Though a plan is a representation of what will happen if events remain under your control, you can never fully control events, nor would you want to.
- Having a plan will help you adjust should any ethical or other hazards arise on the trail.

**Systematically update your plan as your research proceeds.** Avoid overanalyzing or getting stuck in one spot of the plan. A plan with a timeline will help avoid getting you caught up in one aspect of the work—especially the literature review—to the exclusion of the remainder of the research project.

Your plan will evolve as you get better at research; it will change as your inquiry progresses. Expect these changes, and don't panic. Consider the steps of your research plan carefully, but don't make it so detailed that you don't begin your research. Find the balance: do your plan thoroughly and thoughtfully, but focus your energies on the research, not the planning. Some people are very particular in their planning, but never begin. Begin!

**Consider the significant aspects of your study.** When hiking—especially up a mountain—it is always satisfying to stop, catch your breath, and take a look at how far you've come. Sometimes we pull out the trail map to gain some perspective on our progress. As your work progresses, stop and check your own map by revisiting some basic questions.

- What key decisions do you need to make?
- Who can help you?
- What resources do you need?
- What are realistic timelines?
- What outcomes do you really want to see?
- What are the best measures for those outcomes?

If you run into problems, ask someone you respect for advice. You are part of a community of scholars. You have made critical friends—use them. There is also, hopefully, a strong supervisor. Supportive colleagues can offer critical feedback to you during your research implementation. Having a plan also helps you to explain to them what your dilemma is and just where you are on the trail.

**Make certain your central question is important.** The quality of a research study depends mostly on the quality of the research question that frames it. Your own satisfaction with the question you've chosen is the best reason to invest the time, energy, and resources of others. Pursuing a topic because you feel you "should" is always tempting; however, if the topic doesn't truly engage you, you will lack the time, energy and focus needed to complete your work.

# How to Keep Track of Your Data

I remember being faced with a critical life decision that involved the opportunity to move to a new job. If I took it, I would be teaching at a seminary—which is something I really wanted to do—rather than at a secular university. The job was far from Edmonton and meant uprooting my children, and so on. To help make my decision, I went to the most spiritually, guru-ish person I knew and asked him for divine insight.

He listened and said, "Draw a line down a sheet of paper. On one side, put the positives; on the other, put the negatives. Then measure them. Which list is longer?" This was not what I wanted. I wanted some direct tap on the mind of the Creator. Some hocus-pocus stuff with smoke and candles, I guess. I was disappointed. God should reveal Herself in greater majesty than through a line down a piece of paper.

– JIM

To outsiders and newcomers alike, doing research can be a scary idea. To those who do not live with it every day, it seems esoteric and perhaps even a bit majestic. But honestly, it is more like drawing a line down a sheet of paper than it is smoke and candles. If you expected magic, sorry.

Full-time researchers know their craft and have developed systems for their work. One of the most difficult areas of research to get your head around without experience is the systematic tracking of the data for your study. Experience—the one commodity you may not have in abundance—is a good teacher. But if you have never been taught by experience, then what?

One way to overcome the lack of experience is to learn from the methods of those who do research for a living. A classic research article by Miles and Huberman (1984) discusses some simple ways that researchers can keep track of the data they collect. The authors call these methods of keeping up *interim data reduction techniques*.

The real task of research is to create sound from noise. In other words, as a researcher you enter a dynamic world of buzzing activity. Without a plan to order this activity into something that makes sense, it is impossible to understand what is going on. We believe you should draw lines down the centres of papers. In other words, the research techniques or methods that work best are usually the most simple. They are also the most systematic and the easiest to attend to regularly.

Like most good research techniques, the ways Miles and Huberman (1984) "reduce" data to meaningful "knowledge" are actually quite simple. They include:

*Contact summary sheet*
- Here the researcher summarizes a site visit on a single sheet of paper containing information about the people and events, main themes, issues, the research questions addressed, new hypotheses, speculations, and target issues for the next visit. A template can help you to organize these data consistently from one visit to the next.

*Coding*
- With coding, the researcher uses descriptive/high-inference data sheets that look for patterns of behaviour. There are many of these available, or you may make up your own—depending upon what you are looking for. The key here is to come up with systematic descriptors or keywords for the behaviours or incidences that you observe.

*Memoing*
- Memos are brief conceptual looks at insights, puzzles, surprises, emerging explanations, and striking events. The idea here is sort of like keeping a notepad on the table near your bed. When something comes to you, write it down. (You will find that you will be constantly thinking about your research in your off-hours. You don't have to put your life on hold, but when an insight occurs to you, get in the habit of writing it down.)

  Jim supervised a student who would write long emails spelling out the difficulties of analyzing the project. Jim's reaction was to collect and save these emails and send them back when it came time to write about the work. These emails became an excellent set of examples that highlighted the work. The student had, without even realizing it, memoed throughout the project.

*Interim summaries*

- These summaries are short, provisional syntheses of what the researcher knows to date (they may include a review of the findings, a check of the robustness of the supporting data, and so on). Every once in a while—say, on Saturday morning with a latte—stop and write. Make notes about what has occurred to you at that moment. If possible, share your notes with a critical friend and ask for her feedback.

*Questionnaires*

- Questionnaires are used to generate themes and/or points for further study. They are also used to pull together quantitative data so you have some numbers to report. As you know, lots of questionnaires already exist. We have included some examples in this book, but the best ones are those that you use, adapt, or create on your own. These questionnaires—even very simple ones—can be revealing.

  We know a person who, whenever she begins a meeting, asks people to write down answers to two simple questions—with a sentence-long explanation. She is always researching, a little bit at a time, and these questions and answers take only a little time and have proved very revealing.

# Conclusion

You probably could have figured out everything we wrote in this chapter for yourself. Perhaps this seems too easy—like drawing a line down a sheet of paper—or maybe you feel that this must be more complex. But remember that the everyday ways that researchers collect data are really just this simple. It is not the research road that is tough, it is walking that road well that can be difficult. When researchers mess up, it is generally because they are sloppy or inconsiderate, not because of the methodology itself. So walk slowly, be thoughtful as you take in the sights, and devote the time and patience necessary to thoroughly document your research journey.

---

**IMPORTANT: SAVE YOUR WORK!**
Remember to save the results of all your work for later use. Have a special place in your computer or notebook for the results of these data-collection methods. Eventually they add up. You will be surprised, when the time comes, how much you actually have done.

---

# SEVEN

# Collecting
## YOUR DATA

*Set realistic timelines.*

**COLLECTING DATA MEANS DOING THE WORK NEEDED** to find out what you need to find out. Here is where the research rubber meets the road. So far in your research journey, you have chosen your topic of interest, you have considered and decided upon the questions you want to ask, and you have outlined who should be asked these questions. At this stage of data collection, your plans become your actions. You are now at the stage of pulling all these ideas together into an action of discovery. You are ready to collect your data.

In Chapter 6, we spelled out some of the traditional methods for collecting data—and we believe most of these are quite easy to understand. To review, your work should be focused on your specific need, it should be organized in a systematic way, and it should ethically consider the needs of your participants. To us, research is a moral enterprise that should be done with consideration and care.

In Chapter 7, we spell out a number of newer (or less traditional) research methods. And because these might be relatively new to people, we will attempt to give the IKEA version of these. We trust that you will be able to get your head around the methods and use them with confidence. We know the methods may change in their execution, and this is acceptable—in fact, it is common. Adjustments are often required to meet the unique needs of a research study. There is almost always a difference between creating the vision and doing the work. Even the great Canadian literary critic Northrup Frye created an entire concept for a literary genre on contrasting "desire vs. reality." Within our caveat of focused, systematic, and ethical work, changes are acceptable and often necessary.

In Chapter 7, we also offer a sort of compendium of other practical things that might prove helpful to the completion of your research project—things like an introductory letter, a consent form, and some tips about collecting data from other sources. These tips come from a number of years of work, and we hope they will save you frustration and energy.

# Holding a Focus Group

In its simplest sense, a focus group is a collection of people gathered to discuss a specific topic. This group of people will be brought together in one place and asked a question. A small list of questions, focused upon a single topic or issue, is used to generate discussion. The researcher will record the group's discussion, which becomes data. These data can be transcribed and used to understand an issue—much like data collected from interviews. The difference, obviously, is that a larger group of people contributes to the discussion and can, through the act of participating in the group, stimulate a broader range of data than one person being interviewed independently. The information below provides more insight into the workings of focus groups.

## Features of Focus Groups

Here, we look at some of the characteristics of focus groups. It is difficult to classify these as "strengths" or "limitations"—what works well in one situation may be inappropriate in another. Review the points below to consider whether a focus group might work for your research project.

First, focus groups do require a degree of skill to facilitate. If you are going to conduct one yourself, you should be the kind of person who is confident in your people skills—especially your group work skills. A good facilitator is sensitive to the mood of the group and knows how to draw out all participants (some are more reticent than others!). Where tensions arise in the group (and this does happen), a strong facilitator can head them off at the pass or diffuse them once they are out in the open, or even turn those tensions into productive insights. The facilitator should also be able to keep the group on track. This can be a real art: sticking to the agenda of the focus group while allowing sufficient space for ideas to be explored thoroughly.

If this list of responsibilities is a bit overwhelming for you, consider having someone else facilitate your focus group while you participate. You can co-facilitate the group or perhaps act as an observer. If you are freed from the facilitation role by handing it over to a trusted colleague, you may gain a wealth of information with the time and energy you can then devote to direct observation.

Second, focus groups tend to provide in-depth information. In other words, use them to explore one or two topics thoroughly, not to harvest answers to a long list of questions. One mistake we've seen in focus groups is an overambitious agenda. The researcher is dismayed to find out that the focus group has hunkered down on one or two key issues. At the end of the session, he finds he has terrific information, but only on two of the six questions he'd wanted to cover!

If you've hit on a topic that your focus group is really keen to explore, this is probably good news for your research—it means it is important to your stake-holders. However, one issue can dominate a whole focus group session at the expense of other topics you need information on. Before holding your focus group, then, take a look at your research questions and choose the issues that will be most valuable to explore in a group. You can further prioritize by making sure that the important stuff is first on your focus group agenda.

One advantage of focus groups is that they are a quick way to gather a great deal of data from a number of people. They are generally inexpensive and fairly easy to organize, although this is not always the case. A number of past students have found their attempts to organize focus groups hampered by the busy schedules of diverse participants from different locations. You may want to consider sticking to a setting that minimizes logistical difficulties—say, all the participants are from one organization and the group is held during the workday.

Finally, focus groups generate a unique *quality* of data. A good group conversation creates synergy and can reveal insights and generate creative responses that you might not otherwise have the opportunity to learn about. Focus group work has a spontaneity about it that makes its outcomes highly credible. On the dark side, however, poor group dynamics can make for an unpleasant and unproductive experience. Sometimes creativity and spontaneity instead prompt negative or downright unethical conduct by participants.

The direction in which your group falls depends, of course, on your own good judgment about the personality of the group you are dealing with and the sensitivity of the topic that is being discussed. If you feel that you don't know your organization well enough to make these calls, discuss your focus group ideas with a trusted critical friend.

The quality of your focus group experience also depends on the environment you create for it. As a researcher, you should be aware in advance of how this works. Some graduate students have used learning circles to gather data. Perhaps they gather a group of twelve people together into a circle, dim the lights and light candles, put on soft music, and set a relaxed tone for participants. The participants of a learning circle are sort of caressed into conversation. Such a research method is perfect for gathering "caressed conversation," but there should be no surprise that such an approach lends itself more to appreciative inquiry than to critique. Specifically, it may be difficult to gather critical comments this way.

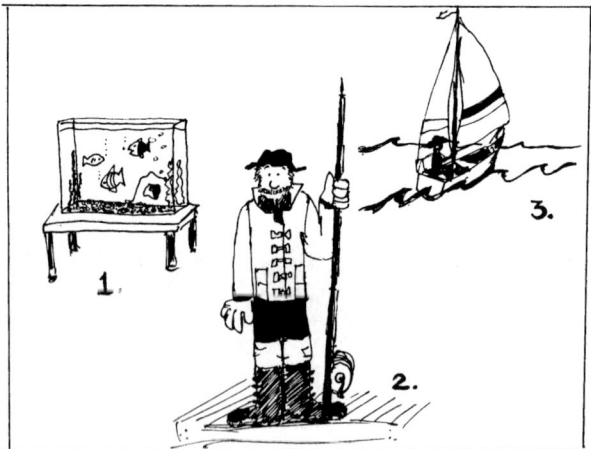

*Ask yourself:*
*1. What data will I collect? 2. How will I collect it?*
*3. Where will I get it?*

This is not a critique of learning circles. It is an illustration of the impact that your chosen environment could have on the integrity of your data. One of Jim's old colleagues attempted to interview junior high students about math anxiety in a room right next to the practice space of a beginning junior high band. There should be no surprise that this researcher found a monstrous intensification of math anxiety. Ask yourself: might there be any correlation between math anxiety and the cacophony of chaos rendered through the rookie reeds of twelve-year-old saxophone players? (That was a rhetorical question. Obviously the answer is "Of course!") Our point is that the environment created to gather data has an effect upon the content and quality of the data themselves. Your task is to create the environment that best suits the data you hope to collect, and then to report how you set up that environment when you write about your study.

## *Creating a Positive Focus Group Experience*

In one-on-one interviews, the privacy of the information shared is relatively straightforward—it is easy to manage the data that are shared because only you and your research subject know what was said in the interview.

The case is quite different in a focus group. Here all participants are witness to one another's perspectives on the research question(s) you are studying. And the more sensitive the topic, the more thought and care you will need to put in to managing the process (the event itself) and the information that emerges from it (your data).

It is important, then, to take a strong leadership role in the facilitation of your focus group by clearly explaining the ground rules for group conduct and the nature of the information shared. It is up to you to establish a constructive discussion in a respectful atmosphere. Consider what steps you will need to take to create a safe environment for your participants and how much lead time you will need to prepare for this. For instance, what information can you share with participants—perhaps in an email or a letter—*before* the event to better prepare them for the experience? Consider the following further guidelines as you structure the discussion.

- Explain ground rules explicitly (perhaps with a preliminary meeting), and be prepared for people to leave if they cannot adhere to the group rules.

- Stress the need for confidentiality and anonymity: what is said in the room stays in the room.
- Offer participants the opportunity to add to ground rules.
- Be considerate of tone, terminology, and organizational culture.
- Consider sensitivity of the topic. Participants are sharing with others, not just the researcher.
- If the discussion is stressful, how do the participants feel once they have left the group? Be sensitive to the possible need for debriefing.
- Create a safe environment for participants: avoid settings of conflict or hierarchy.
- If using a recording device, obtain permission from all participants to do so, in advance of the focus group session if this is possible.
- Otherwise, clearly explain how the data will be recorded and used.
- Don't push too hard: if a participant is holding back despite your encouragement, there is probably a good reason for it.

**Fig. 7.1. Tips for Obtaining Authentic and Trustworthy Data**

- Develop questions using a vocabulary appropriate for your participants.
- Explain how focus group data will be used.
- Immediately after the focus group, build in some time to synthesize the group's perceptions. Begin the process of looking at themes to share with the focus group participants, and verify and validate the content.
- Compare content of the literature review, organizational review, and focus group themes (triangulation).
- Use multiple groups with different individuals on the same topic.
- Use multiple groups with the same individuals on the same topic.
- Create a relaxed atmosphere of psychological safety, group support, and personal openness—an informal, non-judgmental environment motivates simple and direct communication.

### Choosing Focus Group Participants

A provincial government organization we know of recently had a very bad experience with a focus group. Twenty participants were brought together to discuss the effectiveness with which a project, involving numerous other partner organizations, had been carried out. This was a politically sensitive undertaking to begin with, never mind that some of the participating organizations (which had not even been represented in the focus group) were soundly slammed in the report that emerged from this event.

The written results of the focus group barely saw daylight. Critics within the offended organizations correctly charged that the focus group participants—drawn informally and on a volunteer basis by word of mouth—were hardly a fair sampling of project stakeholders. And if they were volunteering for the group, what axes did they have to grind or what agendas of their own did they have to promote? Further, why were so many other partner organizations unaware that the focus group had even taken place? The report literally wound up in the shredder. In fact, there was a greater personal price to pay—during the review meeting, the deputy minister turned on the person who headed the government branch and who was later sent around to the partner organizations to apologize. Then, when this was completed, the branch head was promptly dismissed from his position. There is a lesson here.

The point of this cautionary tale is that poor work can and does happen in the real world, and it will inevitably undermine the credibility of your research. Certainly more ethical and professional protocols could have been undertaken in the above scenario by:

- ensuring that all interested parties had an opportunity to participate
- properly communicating the intent of the focus group
- undergoing a more rigorous selection process
- ensuring that multiple points of view were incorporated
- *not* believing that research is a hammer to clobber others into shape.

Focus group participants should be selected with care and sensitivity. For example, if you know some participants well, how might this affect the dynamics of the group? Will employees feel they can be completely open and honest in front of their managers? Do some participants have agendas or biases that might influence their contributions? Will participants fairly represent others in their cohort? Do participants form a balanced representation of important stakeholders in your research issue? All of these questions bear scrutiny as you are developing your focus group. The trustworthiness of your data is only as good as that of the participants who are providing it.

## More Tips for a Successful Focus Group

- Be sure that your technology works. For example, is the tape recorder functioning properly? Do you have spare batteries and tapes? Will background noise drown out participant voices?
- Use at least two people, one to facilitate and one to record/observe. A third person could observe a particular aspect of the group—for example, focusing solely on participants' body language. Be sure that you have a backup arranged for, in case of illness or unexpected absence.
- Provide food and beverages for participants.
- Know in advance the topics you want to discuss. Perhaps test your open-ended questions beforehand to determine if you will get the kind of information you want to collect.
- Decide what you will do with the information you are gathering. Share this with participants.
- Participants will build on each other's responses. Predetermine useful prompts to draw out information.
- Be prepared to be surprised, and remain flexible.
- Take lots of time ahead to prepare the space. Is the room temperature comfortable? Lighting? Seating?
- Use an odd number of participants.
- Use the first question as an icebreaker.
- Have nametags for participants, and allow them to write in their own name.
- Ask participants to identify themselves before they speak. This will make your transcriber's job—and your subsequent analysis of transcripts—much easier!
- Have lots of extra stuff (pencils, paper, coffee, blank tapes, etc.) ready.

# Open Space Research

*Open Space* is a large-group research technique that works well when the input of many stakeholders is desired. Bryson and Anderson (2000) characterize Open Space by its desire to seek information from as many members of the organization as possible. Often Open Spaces are structured so that data/information is collected as part of an event. Starting as a large group, event agendas are self-organized by those who care most about the information produced, and agenda items are broken into smaller sessions within the room.

## *Characteristics of Open Space Research*

According to Harrison Owen (1997), Open Space operates on four key principles that maximize the impact of the participants. Research participants are informed of these simple principles:

1. Whoever comes are the right people.
2. Whatever happens is the only thing that could have happened.
3. Whenever it starts is the right time.
4. When it's over, it's over.

Owen characterizes Open Space sessions by these points:

- All issues of concern to all in attendance will be raised.
- All issues raised will be discussed to the extent desired.
- All participants will receive a written summary of all proceedings discussed during the session by the end of the session.
- Participants will determine priorities and prepare results-orientated action plans.
- Using the law of "two feet," participants can move to any other discussion anytime they become uninterested, have finished contributing, or simply wish to move on.

The first step when beginning Open Space research is to answer two questions: (1) What information do we need to answer our question? and (2) Who needs to be there to answer this question?

The second step in working with Open Space research is to answer the question: What method allows the best access to the opinions of our constituents? Open Space research, as a technique, facilitates large-group information gathering from those invited to attend the session. This method works for several reasons. First, the approach naturally promotes support and buy-in because participants self-organize and select their interests. Second, Open Space is a grassroots way to rejuvenate participants.

## How to Create an Open Space Research Event

*Preparing your participants*
- Develop any forms you will use with session participants.
- Outline the purpose of the research for participants, and consider how the data will be collected and used. Discuss issues of confidentiality and security, and ways that comments could be deleted from the data for research purposes.

*Preparation details*
- Find a location that works for the anticipated number of attendees.
- Confirm a facilitator.
- Create a list of all the people you wish to attend.
- Create and send out an invitation that outlines the purpose of the session, the date, time, place, focus, and a description of the methodology.
- Notify supervisors, seeking support for staff to rearrange workloads to attend.
- Address the physical requirements of the room, such as chairs, flipcharts, wall space, access to food and beverages, markers, paper, number of personal computers and printers, and access to a copying machine.
- Set up a process for registration of attendees ahead of time and on the day.

*Setting up your research space*
- On the day of the Open Space session, work with the facilitator to set up the space in a large circle, with sufficient chairs for expected participants. Ensure inclusivity.

- Make certain there are flipchart stands, paper, markers, and tape for breakout areas within the main room and separate breakout rooms if the number of participants warrant it.
- Create posters that list the four principles, the law of two feet, and the general question the group will address. Remind participants that they may move to any group they choose.
- Set up sufficient laptops or PCs to allow the results of each concurrent session to be entered by a member of that session. Access to printers and copying facilities is required. The objective is to have a full set of the proceedings of each concurrent session ready for the participants to take away at the end of the session.

*Holding your Open Space event*
- Introduce and welcome participants to the session and state the overall purpose.
- Briefly update participants about why the session was called, its history, and what has influenced it.
- Talk about the purpose of the research and what you hope to accomplish during the Open Space research session. Explain who will see the data and that an individual's participation or input can be excluded from the session's collected data and report if he or she so desires.
- Ask each person to complete the informed consent form. Answer any questions or concerns that arise from this process.
- Open the space by stating the question and how the principles work. Next, ask the group to generate an agenda or discussion group topics by coming into the circle and writing their topics of interest, as each relates to the overarching question, on a piece of paper. Or, brainstorm these topics of interest.
- Assign a time, location, and a leader for each discussion topic articulated on the list. Because the group generates its own agenda items, a facilitator should be ready for any number of topics and must schedule these concurrently during the session. A session will last two to four hours.
- During the small-group process, group members will disperse to the agenda group of their choice. Depending on time, they could attend a second session. Remind group members that they do not have to stay in

a group if it is not interesting to them or if they want to experience a number of groups. Within each group, appoint someone who will stay with the group and create a record of who attended, key topics, and preliminary recommendations. This information should be kept on flipcharts or written directly on a template form in each computer. The length of time allocated to small groups determines how many small-group sessions can occur.

- To conclude the Open Space session, group members are asked to return to the large group. Each person is asked to comment on his or her experience in the space. For the purposes of data collection, someone is chosen to record what the group members said in some detail. This can be a powerful part of the session. There is often a great deal of information and emotion around the support that grows from this community.

- All members are given a copy of the proceeding from all the groups that ran during the Open Space session. Information and preliminary recommendations are available to all members. A final corrected and formatted copy with a transcription of the final circle information should later be sent to all attendees.

- Finally, the working group talks to the group as it closes. This working group can ask for further volunteers to help steer the process. The working group decides when to meet and determines the priorities and recommendations that arise from this first meeting.

## Building an Effective Survey

Entire books are written on the topic of creating surveys that work. For your research, we hope that this brief introduction will provide some guidance if you have not written a survey before.

Writing good surveys is both an art and a science. The art (or instinct) lies in asking the types of questions that genuinely engage the interests and concerns of your participants. The science lies in structuring the survey to get the information you want, and to get it in ways you can somehow measure.

## Common Survey Woes

Make sure that the data you collect are actually helpful to your research. This statement may seem pretty obvious, but you would be amazed at how often surveys generate results that no one can use. There are several reasons for this.

One is that participants can answer in surprising ways. If your question is vague, you may get answers that you cannot classify consistently. For example, suppose you ask the question "What movie did you last see?" You want to know what movie your participants last saw in a *theatre*, but because you weren't specific enough, some respondents list videos they rented and others list movies they watched on TV.

Another reason is that you need to think and work somewhat backwards. Start with your final destination in mind: how are you going to use the results you get? For example, some teenagers are surveyed about their leisure interests so a community can plan future spending. Participants are asked to check off facilities or leisure programs that they would like to see in their area. When the researcher sits down to evaluate his survey results, he realizes that he has no way of measuring which among the choices he gave was most desirable. In fact, some participants had checked off all of the options he provided! Had he thought a little more carefully about how he would use his survey results, he probably would have asked participants to rank their choices from most to least desirable. This would have provided him with more usable data.

Another common mistake is the failure to distinguish between preferences and intent. In the example above, many teens said they would "like" to have a skateboard park in their community. This tells the planners very little. Sure, everyone would like a skateboard park (preference), but how many people would actually use it (intent)? And if so, how often? Participants will often support an idea on paper with no clear idea of how or even if they would be involved in its implementation. Measuring intent in this case is very important.

Take time and expend effort to construct your survey. Get feedback on it before you distribute it. You don't want the frustration of sitting with a stack of only semi-useful data after all the time and trouble you (and your participants) have gone through to gather it.

Finally, be careful with how you use language. In one huge international study, despite the year-long scrutiny of a host of learned researchers, survey questions used the phrase "a couple of times" when the better phrase might have been "one or two times." ("A couple" is an answer you might give an RCMP officer at a check stop when asked how many drinks you've had. Often, what the respondent really means is "I'm falling down, am I?") The response "one or two times" has a more specific, and thus more useful, meaning.

It is wise to have an outsider—meaning, *not* you—read your work, and if possible, actually take your survey. This is called a pilot test, and it helps you avoid some mistakes that can haunt you for the life of your entire project. Always remember, it is better to take five minutes to address a problem early in the process than to spend hours trying to resolve it after the survey has been implemented. (The same is true, by the way, with citations in your review of literature.) Why are we saying this? Because we have been forced to pay for our research sins, and we want to help you avoid these same problems.

## Types of Questions You Can Ask

The options available for survey questions can generally be divided into two categories: close-ended and open-ended questions. Each has advantages and disadvantages that should be considered.

**Close-ended questions.** Close-ended questions restrict the participant to a range of responses that you, the researcher, have made available. They are most useful when you need to measure (i.e., quantify) the data you gather and use it to generate statistics. No doubt you recognize many of these types of questions from surveys you have taken yourself.

**List questions.** These provide a number of items or statements, usually accompanied by some sort of checkbox. Participants may be asked to select as many items as apply or to rank the items on the list in order of importance. Here are some examples of list questions.

*Recently, the board of directors at Ye Olde Blacksmith School of Yore bandied about some suggestions for increasing enrollment. In your opinion, which of these suggestions should the board pursue further? Check as many as apply.*

\_\_ *tuition caps*
\_\_ *target older students*
\_\_ *charm school for instructors*
\_\_ *presentations at high schools*
\_\_ *free beer in student lounge*
\_\_ *improve practicum program*
\_\_ *promote scholarships available*
\_\_ *daycare program for students with children*

*The Ye Olde Blacksmith School of Yore is considering standardizing its final exams for blacksmithing students. In your opinion, which of the following formats is most appropriate? Please rank your responses from 1 to 5, writing "1" next to the most appropriate, "2" next to the second most appropriate, and so on.*

\_\_ *essay exam*
\_\_ *practical exam*
\_\_ *oral exam*
\_\_ *short-answer/multiple-choice exam*
\_\_ *no final exam: evaluate a year-end portfolio*

**Exclusive categories.** These questions require participants to select one and only one category into which they fit. Common examples are those questions that ask you to select the age range or income range you fit into. For example:

*What is your annual income? (Check the income range that applies to you.)*
\_\_ *$10,000 or less*
\_\_ *$10,001–$24,999*
\_\_ *$25,000–$49,999*
\_\_ *$50,000–$89,999*
\_\_ *$90,000 or more*

**Likert scale–type questions.** These are usually used to survey beliefs, perceptions, and attitudes. You've probably seen these questions before; for example, they will show "Very Satisfied" at one end of the continuum and "Very Dissatisfied" at the other end. For example:

---

*(Check one category). I kiss my children goodnight:*

| **ALWAYS** | **OFTEN** | **SOMETIMES** | **RARELY** |
|---|---|---|---|
| (Every day) | (3–4 days a week) | (1–2 days a week) | (Less than once a week) |
| ✔ | | | |

---

Close-ended questions have one major disadvantage: they provide no opportunity for the participant to identify her own issues and concerns. Say, for instance, that you ask your research participants to rank the "Top Five Things That Make Me Crabby at Work" from a list you've provided. On your list you've included: no toilet paper in the washrooms, smelly air conditioning, and when the copier runs out of toner. Yet the biggest problem the staff have at this organization (and the one you did NOT include on your list) is the incessant elevator music piped into the office all day long. Your participants cannot tell you about this because their most important issue does not show up as an item on your checklist.

One way to help work around this problem is to create an "Other" category and ask participants to explain what their "Other" is. While responses won't be consistent from participant to participant, this measure can help you to catch things you might have missed.

Further, you can always combine closed-ended questions and open-ended questions. Here's an example of two possible questions to add.

*After filling out the survey, do you feel that any important questions were missed? If so, tell us what the survey failed to have you answer.*

*In assessing your organization, what does an insider know that an outsider should know but cannot?*

**Open-ended questions.** Because of the problem we've just described, it is always a good idea to include some open-ended questions in your survey. These invite your participants to respond in a more in-depth and individualized manner.

In open-ended questions, use questions that ask "How?" "Why" and "In what ways?" These encourage thoughtful responses. Avoid questions that prompt yes/no or single-word answers. See the sample questions below and the responses they generate. Which response gives you more useful information?

The WRONG way     *Has the department been helpful to you in the past six months?*
                  – No, not really.

The RIGHT way     *In what ways have you found this department helpful during the past six months? Please describe any experiences with this department (positive or negative) in detail.*
                  – The department hasn't been very helpful to me. When I phone for information, they don't return my calls for days.

While open-ended questions are intended to provide your participants with more latitude in their responses, you may still need to direct them somewhat. Sometimes we need some prompting or some triggers to recall important information. In other words, be specific enough that you are still targeting the information you really need.

The WRONG way     *Have you had any problems with the office's facilities in the past six months?*
                  – No.
                  (Note: The term "facilities" is vague, and the participant doesn't really know what it means.)

| The RIGHT way | *In what way(s) could we improve the coffee area for staff?* |
| | – Furniture would be nice. |
| | |
| | *In what way(s) could we improve the library/research area for staff?* |
| | – Move the book stacks by the window farther apart. They are hard to access. |

Open-ended questions have some disadvantages, however. First, as you've probably guessed, the responses are often highly individualized and may be difficult to classify or categorize. While site-based research lends itself well to the qualitative data gathered in open-ended questions, there may still be areas where you want measurable, consistent responses. In these cases, do not use open-ended questions.

Also, you can really burn out your participants with a long survey of open-ended questions, which require more time and effort to fill out. If you overload your participants with questions that require lengthy responses, the quality (and quantity) of these responses is likely to go down. By page three, you'll be noticing lots of two- or three-word responses or questions that haven't been answered at all. Limit the number of open-ended questions you use. You might also break it up a bit by interspersing open-ended and close-ended questions.

**Fig. 7.2. Summary: Survey Writing Tips**

- Write in language that your participants can easily understand. Keep it simple.
- Define any terms that your participants may be unfamiliar with. Avoid jargon.
- In the introduction, explain the purpose of the survey. Give participants some idea of how long it will take to complete.
- Ask one question at a time. Even in a series of related questions, it is best to create one response item per question.
- Plan in advance how you will you use the information you've gathered.
- Test your survey, or review it with a critical friend or small pilot group before mass circulation.
  - Does it make sense?
  - Is it easy to fill out?
  - Is all the information useful and relevant?
- Frame sensitive questions carefully. Even anonymous participants can be touchy about admitting to negative thoughts, feelings, or behaviours.
- Remember to thank participants for their time.

# Conducting Interviews

Surveys are useful tools for quickly and consistently collecting data to help your project. However, the trade-off for this efficient breadth of data may be a loss of depth in responses. For this reason, researchers often find it worthwhile to supplement the information they gather from surveys with the more detailed, nuanced, and often more personal insights that can be gathered from interviews.

## *Choosing an Interview Structure*

Interviews may be as structured or unstructured as you would like them to be. The important points to consider (as always when gathering data) are the practical constraints of your project (you may not have time to learn every subject's life story) and how you are planning to use the information you gather.

**More structure: A semi-structured interview.** Say, for instance, you want to investigate the learning experiences of your fellow workers in a recent all-day

Team Building workshop. Here you are able to use a fairly structured interview format because all of your interviewees attended the same workshop. Further, you are interested to see that different people can have widely varying perceptions of the same events. The more structured interview allows you to capture this.

**Less structure: An emergent interview.** In another case, a researcher may be gathering historical information about an organization. Here, he is only looking for a feel for what has been done in the past and will look for themes later when he reviews his data. Also, the people he is interviewing come from a wide variety of backgrounds within the organization and have served in different capacities for different lengths of time and through different eras of the organization. In this case, a very unstructured interview would be appropriate.

**Fig. 7.3. Interview structures.**

| More Structure | Less Structure |
|---|---|
| • more consistent responses<br><br>• easier to spot trends, code responses, and analyze results | • more difficult to code and analyze results across many participants because interview contents may vary considerably |
| • less important to build relationship with interviewee | • allows the interviewer and the interviewee more opportunity to build a trusting relationship |
| • less rich, but more efficient and potentially less time-consuming | • can be less formal and more conversational |
| • provides the researcher with greater control over the shape and direction of the interview | • allows the researcher to encounter and explore ideas and insights initiated by the research participant |
| • easier for those with less interviewing experience | • requires good interviewing skills, strong people skills |

## *Preparing Your Research Subjects*

One option for a more structured interview is to provide in advance a list of the questions you will be asking. The list sets up a consistent structure for the interview and allows participants to think ahead—if they choose—in preparation for the conversation. Participants are also fully informed of what to expect, which can help put them at ease in the interview. They are also able to make an informed decision should they choose to opt out of the interview. (Remember that providing this choice is a tenet of your research ethics.)

## Sample Interview Questions

Below is a sample of interview questions for a research project that explored possible mentorship models for the Edmonton YMCA. This student accompanied her list of questions with a pre-interview written survey, thus combining some qualitative and some quantitative data in her study.

> *Dear Participant:*
>
> *Thank you for your interest in participating! The following list of questions will be used to guide our conversation during your personal interview. Do not fill in either Part 1 or Part 2 of this form, as notes will be taken for you. However, it may help to jot down your thoughts and ideas on a separate sheet of paper.*

*INTERVIEW QUESTIONS*

1.  What is your job/position at the Edmonton YMCA?
2.  What do you like about working at the Edmonton YMCA?
3.  What don't you like about working at the Edmonton YMCA?
4.  What concerns do you have regarding your workplace environment?
5.  Are you aware of why employees have left?
6.  How do you think retention can be improved and why? What needs to change?
7.  Based on your experiences with being part of a self-directed team, give an example of a challenge the team had. Describe the challenge and what the team did in response.

8. Describe a situation in which you were able to build a relationship with a member of management, even when you felt the situation was difficult and the odds were against you.
9. What is your perception of the management mentorship effectiveness?

## Tips for Conducting Interviews

- Set a timeframe, but not a stringent one.
- Allow the participant to elaborate a little to enrich the conversation and the results.
- Note your observations about body language if it impacts the study.
- Keep your personal feelings and opinions at bay to avoid contaminating the data.
- People are glad to help. Just give them the opportunity to stop or to say no at any time, and respect it.
- Choose a quiet, private location for the interview.
- Set up the interview well in advance. It is hard for subjects to participate while they are working or if they have to use their break to help you.
- Set up interviews with times and dates so your subject is ready for the interviewer.

# Observation

We think that observation is perhaps the most fun—and in many ways the most informative—aspect of research. It is people-watching with a research purpose!

On the downside, observation can be time-consuming. Perhaps you will not spend the sort of time Jane Goodall did with her apes. (When her institute wrote the book *Forty Years at Gombe: A Tribute to Four Decades of Wildlife Research, Education, and Conservation*, they really meant forty years.) Still, it will take some time to do observation well. It is seldom possible to get a feel for a situation after only one or two observation sessions.

Even if observation is not your main research method, it can play an important part, and you should work to create some "formal" ways to note your observations (such as forms or templates you can use in a practical manner). Creating forms for keeping track of your research is an idea we will keep repeating—we hope you are listening. Many students keep personal journals during their research projects, and observations can be recorded in these journals simply as a way of building insight and context for the study. Some simply spend an hour with coffee each Saturday morning to reflect on the past week, keeping an unedited log of activities on some space on their hard drive. Some students report back to their supervisor each week in a regular fashion, and these reports serve as a formal way to track research "stuff."

Or you may decide that observations will form part of your research methodology, in which case you will need to be careful, systematic, and rigorous about what and how you record. But however you use observation, it will enrich your work. The following information should help you to hone your watching and listening skills.

**Study the research setting using all your senses.** When real estate agents hold open houses, they often suggest that their sellers burn candles or bake bread to make the house smell good. Interior designers may pour over colour charts while choosing a look for a corporate office that suggests it is eco-friendly. The atmosphere of a restaurant—its smells, appearance of uncleanliness, and suspicious lack of other customers—may make you want to turn and run out the door! We use information from our senses to form our responses to environments, and we study these environments in turn to help us form impressions of what kind(s) of people hang out there. A rich description of the physical space where your observations are taking place can lend insight about the people who occupy that space.

Don't forget, too, that the timing of your observations is an important aspect of your setting. An organization's members may behave very differently during peak season than during down season. As another example, any school teacher will tell you that the class first thing in the morning is very different from the class just before lunch!

**Study the research participants.** Researchers often work best from structure. The following questioning pattern provides a way to organize your insights. If you can answer the following questions, you might then develop a systematic way to gain insight into the people who are your participants. Remember, many of these questions may be too digging and may not jibe with your research needs, but they will give you a sense of what you might look for.

1. What does the person look like? What physical appearances stand out? Do any of these appearances reflect organizational culture? (Watch for posture, movements, dress, and physical features.)
2. Does the person utilize esoteric or organizational language or uncommon expressions of speech? Are there odd ways of saying things that are part of the organization?
3. Does the person behave (have habits or special interests) in ways that reflect organizational thinking?
4. What makes this person special, and is this related to the organization in which the person lives and works? Why does this person stand from the crowd?
5. What physical evidence can you find that tells you something about the person or the organization? (Think as an anthropologist or archaeologist would. Don't forget photos, collections of items, things on desks, or magazines lying around.)

**Separate observations from judgments and inferences.** An old maxim for writers is "Show, don't tell." This means to write so that readers can gain insight rather than be told. Here is a simple example.

*The patient was upset by the visit from her family.*

*The patient was pale and shaking after her visitors left. Whereas she was smiling and talkative earlier that day, I now found her uncommunicative. I stopped in three times that afternoon to invite her to talk, but she insisted that she was tired and wanted to sleep.*

Both of the above examples describe the same situation. It is obvious to us that the second does a better job. In the first, we are left to ask (1) how the observer knew the patient was upset, and (2) how the observer came to the certainty that it was the visit with her family that had caused this upset. The second takes the extra time to spell out the circumstances and the results. It is better writing in that it is more revealing of the research situation, and it is also more interesting to read.

The second example simply describes—with good detail—what the observer observed. The *meaning* of what has been observed is not assumed here; it is left for future analysis. Suppose, for instance, that after several more interactions with this patient, the nurse in question begins to believe that the patient is suffering from depression or some other mood disorder. In this case, her earlier belief that the patient's family relationships were to blame is no longer so certain. Yet in the first example, it is stated as a certainty—as a fact. Remember, once you write something in a categorical manner—as if there is no other choice—you must take responsibility for what you have written. It is difficult to go backward and remember and rework the insights you have gained.

Hopefully, this example illustrates the danger of making too many early assumptions about what you are observing. A way around this is simply to be conscious that making observations—what you can see, touch, or hear—is a separate process from *inferring* or judging what those observations mean.

To get around this potential problem, you can make a point of separating your observations from your judgments in your notes. Create two columns on your sheet of paper. On the left side, note your empirical (i.e., what you can experience with your senses) observations. On the right, note your own reflections, questions, or thoughts about what your observations mean.

**Fig. 7.4. An example of research notes that clearly separate observation from judgment.**

| Observation | Reflections/Notes |
|---|---|
| Tess complained of being sleepy a lot on this shift, but she did not actually sleep very much—was awake every time I checked in on her. No change in her meds. | Is Tess suffering from a mood disorder? She seems to change lots from day to day, for no reasons that I can see. Or is it just because of this extended hospital stay? I wonder what she is like at home. |

## Fig. 7.5. Tips for Observing As a Researcher

- Study the setting using all your senses. Use descriptive words to document your perceptions.
- If you are looking within your own organization, try to make the familiar strange. Imagine yourself as a complete newcomer to this setting, and take a fresh look at all of those subtle "background elements" that you've probably come to take for granted.
- For each thing you notice, ask "Does this mean something?"
- Study your participants. Ask and answer questions that reveal both the person and the organization in which the person "lives." Who are they in terms of age, gender, social class, and ethnicity? How are they dressed?
  How do they interact? What are their conversations about?
- Study the events. Differentiate between special events and common daily events. Look for the subtle little acts that make up each event.
- Study people's gestures. How do people show attitude and emotion? What gestures are used, and why?
- Focus on behaviours and concrete details. These are easier to work with later when you want to start working your field notes into categories for analysis.

– ADAPTED FROM GLESNE AND PESHKIN 1992

## Writing a Cover Letter

Regardless of the method you choose—surveys, interviews, or requests to make observations—it is necessary to write a cover letter that provides as much information as possible to your potential participants. This is simply a practical consideration, and one you may not have much experience with. A cover letter ensures that participants have many of their questions answered consistently and in advance of the research conducted. This has two advantages: first, it saves you time because you are not answering and reanswering many of these questions in your scheduled session. Second, it is ethical to inform your participants as much as possible of your research intentions. Your advance notice can also put your subjects at ease; they will know exactly what they can expect.

Attached are sample cover letters for interviews with organizations and individuals. In either case, the letter informs your research participants of:

- your credentials and your reasons for doing the site-based research project
- the purpose and topic of your study and why the individual's or organization's input would be valued
- the general format of the interview or survey you will be conducting (length of time required, types of questions that will be asked)
- any other information that your subject(s) might need to prepare.

More specifically and at the time of the interview/survey, you should have participants sign a consent form that outlines the conditions under which the survey will take place. For both yourself as researcher and your participants, outline rights, responsibilities, and obligations. For more ideas about ethical considerations that might shape your letter, go back and consult Chapter 3.

**Fig. 7.6. An example of a cover letter to an organization.**

October 10, 2004

H. Davidson, VP Public Relations

Re: "Best Case Practice" for Attracting and Retaining Short-term Blacksmiths

Dear Harley Davidson,

Thank you for agreeing to meet with me regarding the "Best Case Practice" interview arranged by my mother. As you are aware, your organization has been identified as having successful blacksmith employment practices. This letter provides you with some background information prior to our meeting and also shares the interview questions.

My name is Cale McKale, and I am a university student from Manyberries, Alberta. I am conducting a study on the best practices for retaining blacksmiths. This study is in partial fulfillment of the requirements for the Master of Arts degree I am pursuing at Blackberry University. As part of the study, information is collected from organizations with a successful history of blacksmith employment.

The interview will take approximately one hour. All identifiable responses will be kept anonymous and confidential, and will be used in a best practice final report as one part of a research project. I will be the only person besides my mom who will have access to any identifiable individual responses, in order to analyze the data for the final study report.

It is anticipated that a final report for this project will be available by the end of May 2004. A copy of the final report will be available to view at your request. Participation in this research is voluntary, and you may withdraw at any time.

If you have any questions please call me at (250) 250-2222 or email my.mother@herhouse.com. If you have any questions as a research participant, please feel free to contact my mom at home: (413) 413-4123.

Your time and input would be greatly appreciated. Thank you in advance for your consideration.

Sincerely,

Cale McKale

## Fig. 7.7. An example of a cover letter to an individual participant.

October 3, 2004

Dear Potential Research Participant,

You are invited, on a purely voluntary basis, to participate in a research study that investigates the systemic effects of project-based teaching on student achievement.

I am conducting this study in partial fulfillment of the requirements for a Master of Arts degree from the University of Alberta. The information gathered from this questionnaire will be used in combination with other data to identify the holistic effect on students' learning as a result of project-based teaching. The knowledge gained from this study will be provided to undergraduate teacher candidates at the University of Alberta as an aid to curriculum planning in their pre-service education program.

Your opinions are important for this study. I am in the process of analyzing the data gathered in this study. I hope to gain insight into ways our pre-service instruction might be improved.

Your participation is completely voluntary, and you need only answer those questions which you feel comfortable addressing. This questionnaire is expected to take approximately fifteen minutes. All responses will be kept completely anonymous and strictly confidential. Only the researcher will have access to the individual responses to analyze data and prepare a final report. Dr. Jim Parsons from the University of Alberta is my academic advisor, and I can provide you with details, if you wish, to contact him regarding this study.

If you wish to receive information on the findings, I will gladly make them available to you once the study is complete. Data gathered will be kept in a locked filing cabinet for five years under the possibility it might be used for further research. After five years, all information in hard copy will be shredded and any electronic data will be destroyed.

By completing this survey, it is understood that you agree to having read the above information and are freely consenting to participate in the study. If you have any questions, please contact me at 1–222–222–1978 (weekends) or 1–222–222–5225 (work) or via the email addresses provided above.

By Tuesday, please seal your completed survey in the self-addressed envelope provided and return it to me, or send the completed questionnaire by email to wyatt.hurtzburg@holyspirits.ca. Your support in this research initiative is greatly appreciated, and I thank you for your time, input and effort in this endeavour.

Sincerely,

Wyatt Hurtzburg

**Fig. 7.8. An example of a consent form for research participants.**


Blackberry University
**Research Participant Consent Form**


"Best Case Practices" for Blacksmith Employment Research Project

Title: **What Organization Factors Optimize Retention of Blacksmiths?**

Investigator: Cale McKale, MA Candidate
(Master of Arts, Traditional Crafts, Blackberry University)

Project Supervisor: Dr. Mig Snosrap


Dear Participant,

Please read the following carefully. Your signature below indicates that you consent to participate in the above-named study, which will follow the methods described below:

- The interview will take approximately one hour.

- All interview data and conversations will be kept strictly confidential unless otherwise advised.

- Your participation is voluntary and anonymous. You can withdraw at any time. The researcher is the only individual who will know of your participation.

- The interview will be taped, and you will have the right to ask that the tape be stopped at any point during the interview. If this happens, the transcripts will be destroyed and tapes erased at that point.

- The researcher will personally transcribe the tapes. Identifiable information, tapes, and transcripts will be kept locked and secure in the researcher's home and will be destroyed once the study is complete (May 2005). Interview transcripts will not contain the real names of participants. You will be identified throughout the research notes by a code number.

- You will be given a copy of the transcripts to review, verify, and revise at your discretion.

- The data from your interview/survey will be one part of a thesis and may also be used in other forms such as professional journals, always maintaining the same standards of confidentiality and anonymity.

- There will be no monetary compensation for participating.

- A summary of the study results will be made available to you at the end of the project (May 2005) upon request.

- You should feel free to ask for clarification or new information throughout your participation in this study.

If you have further questions concerning matters related to this research, please contact Cale McKale collect at (250) 250–2222 or email cale@caleshouse.com. If you have any questions regarding your rights as a research participant, please feel free to contact my mother at home by phoning (800) 444–9209.


Participant (*please print name*)  _____

Signature _____     Date _____


Researcher (*please print name*)     ___CALE MCKALE_____

Signature _____     Date _____

# EIGHT

# Analysis:
## MAKING SENSE OF YOUR DATA

*A focus group is a collection of people
brought together to discuss a specific topic.*

IT IS NOT ENOUGH TO SIMPLY COLLECT YOUR DATA and leave them there for others to make sense of. First, you have to organize it; second, you have to analyze it. All of this may seem new, but honestly, you already have the skill set to complete this task. Organizing your data is not so different from working with a review of literature. If you have already done that, you will have a sense of how to shape the data that you have. So now that you are up to your ears in data, what should you do?

# Whacks and Whacks of Data...Now What?

Let us begin simply. The first question is What do your data look like? The answer, in its most simple form, is that data are generally presented in audio, video, or textual formats. Generally, audiovisual data come from tapes of interviews or conversations or meetings, and the first thing that most researchers do is reshape this sound into text. Simply stated, you are moving from noise (the scientific sense of *noise* is "sound without a recognizable pattern") to meaningful sound (you are creating or recognizing patterns in the "noises" you have collected).

As mentioned, most researchers almost immediately turn sound into text—and many, simply without thinking, send it to an outsider (a transcriber, for example) to create that text. (Remember, any time you use an outside person to work with your data, you should review confidentiality requirements with them. Most professionals understand the importance of research ethics, but you should take this precaution anyway.) There are alternatives to working exclusively with data in text form. In fact, there may be good reason to leave recorded sound as sound, and to shape it in that form.

For example, if you are interviewing participants about a controversial organizational issue, the words used have a definitional meaning but they may also carry an inflected meaning. Certainly, you have been in places where you have been speaking with a person whose language has simply dripped with irony. In that case, the words alone do not tell you the entire story. Or sometimes it is impossible or difficult for practical reasons—including time and money—to transcribe tapes.

## Using Taped or Videotaped Data

Recently, Jim has encouraged some of his graduate students to leave the work in its sound format. His instruction is to listen to the tapes three times.

1.   Listen to all the tapes in as short a time as possible to corroborate the sense you had of what was happening as you were conducting your interviews. While you listen, take notes about what themes or categories you should use to organize your work.
2.   The second time you listen, reclarify your themes in your head and take notes that would help you explain these themes to your readers.

3. Listen to find the direct quotes you want to use to highlight the meanings of your themes—these are the grounds for creating your theories for your work.

After you have completed these steps, go ahead and write up your work.

## *Working With Textual Data*

There a number of forms that textual data might take. Some of these include:

- pictures or drawings
- short answers (survey responses, for example)
- longer answers (open-ended surveys, for example)
- transcribed conversations or interviews
- notes from a variety of sources.

Using pictures or drawings is rare, but it does happen. For example, a researcher might be doing a study of corporate logos or icons. A person might be doing a text analysis of the photos an organization uses to highlight its programming. But even when using pictures or icons, a typical next step would be to create text about these photos or icons. Specifically, as you study the pictures or icons you would take textual notes about what they mean. The text you generate becomes the data you will work to organize. At this point the researcher is back to shaping words from textual responses into meaning.

Surveys, either closed-ended or open-ended, are rather easy to organize into meaning. Typically, if you give a ten-question survey to one hundred workers in an organization, the easiest way to organize the responses is to provide a short introduction to the work and then to list the questions, one at a time, and quantify the responses. This would be as true with short-answer (choose *a*, *b*, *c*, *d*, or *e*) responses as with more open-ended notes. When reporting these, typically one chapter in your final report would discuss the count of the responses (the What? of your research findings) and the next chapter would focus on analyzing the responses (to say what the responses mean—the So what? of your research findings).

Transcribed interviews or conversations provide the researcher with large hunks of text to review. However, the process of shaping the meaning of these is only slightly different from the processes we have outlined earlier. (Note that so much of research is doing things correctly rather than doing them creatively.)

1. Read the transcripts through to see that you have your head around what was happening.
2. Read the transcripts to discover your themes or categories for shaping the data into meaning.
3. Read the transcripts to choose examples for citing.

Notes may take several forms. Some of these include posters, journals, emails, memos, and so on. Again, you might reshape the notes—posters that are artifacts of a focus group newsprint session, for example—into more workable (size-wise, for example) units. However, the process and order of organizing the content for meaning would remain similar.

1. Read for general understanding.
2. Read for organizational shaping (categories).
3. Read for specific examples that illustrate important points.

In so many ways, organizing data differs little from organizing the notes you took when you completed your literature review. At the point of work, the text looks the same. And at the point of shaping, the process is remarkably similar. The end result is also the same—you are arranging bits and pieces of text into units that make your research clear and meaningful to your readers.

## Interpreting Your Findings: The "So What?"

The directions implicit in the work above dealt with the What? of your study. *What* did you find when you searched? *What* insights did the participants provide for your work?

The next step is the So what? At this point, you are working to provide insight for those who are reading your work. You've probably made all sorts of observations and speculations as you've conducted your research; hopefully you've recorded lots of notes to yourself about what you've seen and considered. You can now use these notes, and your "latte reflections," just like any of the other textual data we've already discussed.

1. Review for overall impressions.
2. Slot your thoughts (as best you can) into an organizing framework.
3. Draw out specific examples...you know the process!

Beyond this, it is difficult to provide a simple recipe for analyzing data. There is no special set of directions for this work, except to be systematic, organized, honest, considerate, and careful. However, we can offer this advice: in our work, we have seen two sorts of errors. The first is daring to say too much with your data, and the second is daring to say too little.

Because the task is to move from gathered data to meaning, daring to say too much can happen when the data do not support the analysis. One reason for this extra verbiage is that the data were weak and the researcher wants desperately to move to sharing insights that were neither present nor could be supported from the findings. Another would be when the researcher carries biases—either conscious or unconscious—into the research and onto the analysis. Often it is not that the researcher intends to allow his perspective to overwhelm the findings; instead, it is that it is very difficult to let go of hegemonic perspectives that only provide a narrow, predetermined translation of the data. These are reasons to utilize your supervisor as you undertake your research project. Simply stated, it helps to talk things through with a trusted advisor.

Perhaps a more common problem is a researcher who is too cautious. Sometimes the data "say" more than the researcher shows. It is understandable to be cautious, because the opposite problem—overanalysis—seems too much a risk. Our suggestion is to be daring, but you must be able to point to the footprints (data) that showed where to follow the trail. Explain how you came to the conclusions that you did. If you can do this, your insights should be relatively safe ones. Again, this is an area where a critical friend—including your supervisor—might be extremely helpful. Talk about what you have seen, and listen to the insights of others who also care to look at your work.

Our encouragement is to take time during your research project to track your thoughts and ideas and to share those with those with whom you are working. Earlier in this book, we have encouraged some forms of personal note taking. These include memos, journals, emails back and forth to your network of critical friends, and so on. If you avail yourself to take notes throughout the process, our experience is that those notes will come in helpful when it is time to write up analysis of data during the final report. We encourage you to systematically keep a copy (perhaps by sending one to yourself or as part of your sent email records) of those thoughts you have had about your work. One of the best things about your university compatriots is that they become ready and willing friends. Now, organize the troops for the mutual benefit of your own and their own work!

---
**CASE STUDY**
---

## Fig. 8.1. Organizing and Interpreting Data

*Here's an example of the sort of data you might draw from a particular study, along with some suggestions about how they might be written up in a report.*

Your organization, located in northern British Columbia, would like to create a booklet that provides readers with both the "content" message they are trying to impart and visual images appropriate to this content. Five years ago, the organization hired a consulting firm to create a booklet that might communicate its purpose and services to potential clients. They ask you to take a look at this booklet and to write a short report. They are not quite happy with the work, but are unsure why. As one organizational leader notes, "It just seems wrong somehow."

When you look at the work, you read it carefully. Your initial look shows you that there are several "parts" to the booklet. First, there is a text that is broken into several sections. For example, one part tells the history of the company; another outlines the organizational vision. Plus, there is a second part of the booklet: the photos. Some of these photos show people who work at the plant, and some show the organization in action. Third, there is a series of charts that seem tailored to convey the company's success.

You first study the language of the text and decide that it is excessively formal. This, to you, is a problem because the readers of the booklet are rural northern British Columbians. Most of them are labourers, and few have a university education. When you study the photos, you see two things: again, most of the photos don't seem to reflect the experiences of the readers; they show the high-management sorts of people, quite nattily dressed in shirts and ties. Plus, most are men, and most are white. This hardly corresponds with the rank and file of the organization for whom the booklet is written, many who are Aboriginal and many who are women. Perhaps some have never worn a tie—ever.

The charts are, from this perspective, also problematic. They seem more intended to outline the global than the local, and the possibility of corporate merger more than the needs of those workers within the organization. There are other things you note, but this theme keeps pounding its way onto the pages, and your sense is that the consultant firm that created the booklet five years ago just simply missed the audience.

So how do you organize the data? A report may be written using an outline something like this:

*Text*
- reading level (examples)
- formal language and alternatives

*Photos*
- gender, class, and ethnicity
- activities portrayed

*Charts and Data*
- ease of comprehension?
- usefulness of data presented?

Once the data from the brochure are used to create this basic outline, additional data from other sources can easily be incorporated into the categories. Say, for instance, that someone conducted a focus group on the brochure. Comments of participants could be sorted as above and used to elaborate on the observations that emerge from the focus group.

# How to Know Your Findings Are Accurate

All researchers must ultimately ask themselves, "Can I trust my findings?" Regardless of your specific research project and methods, you can have more confidence in the accuracy of your results when you use a number of different data sources. Unless they are really goofy, the use of multiple sources—triangulation—always gives you a more comprehensive picture of what you are studying.

## *Triangulating Your Data*

The term **triangulation** is used quite commonly in research. However, it first emerged from the daily practice of sailors and surveyors. In practical terms, one's position was always measured in reference to another place. But it was never enough to use one or two points of reference to ascertain where you were—location was best understood by studying it as the intersection of three points. Using proper equipment and careful tools for measurement, sailors were able to circumnavigate the world and surveyors were able to accurately draw lines and boundaries. In a world where accuracy was a life-and-death matter, being a few degrees off could mean being lost forever.

Perhaps the situation is not as "life or death" now, but researchers still need solid and useful points of reference. However, triangulation cannot be thought of literally as three sources of data or three methods—only a novice or exceedingly literal researcher would make such a claim. It is the concept of using a variety of data-gathering sources to help ensure reliability that is key, not a specific sense of three methods. In research terms (as considered by Denzin 1978), triangulation simply has come to mean that researchers use different sets of data, different types of analyses, and different theoretical perspectives to study one particular phenomenon. One perspective is just that: one perspective. In a research study, different points of view are studied in order to situate the research for both the researcher and the reader of his or her work. Thoughtful consideration and agreement is a keystone to judgment. For this reason, juries in criminal trials are made up of more than one person.

*Each researcher views and interprets data differently.*

A researcher carefully considers and chooses the particular points of reference that will help her to triangulate the study. These points—perspectives or methods—in and of themselves can also tell readers much about how they should locate the research for themselves, and how much they can generalize from this research to answer questions that arise from their own interests. As a simple example, if a researcher studies only women or children—yet uses several methods to study these groups—the research may be solid and useful, but only insofar as it pertains to women and children. It would still be good research, but it would not be satisfactory in and of itself to address the particular needs of men within an organization. The same could be said of research studies that are limited to positional status (executives) or culture (European) or geography (in the southern USA) or time (completed prior to 1975).

As mentioned, sailors and surveyors triangulated so that they might locate where they were in relation to other points. Similarly, in research, triangulation helps the researcher locate and make sense of the meaning discovered by the participants or in the situation or activity being studied. But it's important to point out that one certain perspective in triangulation that must not be forgotten: that of the person doing the research! There has never been a researcher who has not had a perspective on the study being completed! That is why good qualitative research (in fact, all good research) begins with as careful a description of the researcher as possible. The sailor's location is always part of the triangulation, and the researcher's perspective is always part of the research.

Sagor (1992) describes perspectives as "three independent windows" on the problem studied. We have adapted the following example from his work:

> Say a researcher wants to study the use of cooperative work within an organization. That researcher might choose to study the texts within the organization (booklets, memos, department meeting agendas, etc.), have a colleague observe the functions of an office, have a manager evaluate her own performance on videotape, and have another colleague interview the workers. If all these windows on one cooperative work "report" the same picture, that picture is likely a valid portrait of the organization. But suppose the manager rated her leadership as inspiring, while the workers saw it differently? These differences—potential sources of further inquiry—would be lost if a single measure were used.

As Sagor's example shows, triangulation gives a researcher more faith in the findings, especially when different sources agree. When different data sources show discrepancies, more study and data collection are required before one can have confidence in the results.

Triangulating data sources does demand more planning and more data gathering to provide multiple, independent windows on the study, but if you want your research to be credible, triangulation is essential.

## Reliability and Validity

When you are reading research, you will often come across the terms *reliability* and *validity*. Each of these ideas is crucial to the conduct of good research. All professional researchers believe that they should conduct research "considerately." This means that they must address both validity and reliability.

- For **validity**, we ask, "Does the research method do what it says it will do?"
- For **reliability**, we ask, "Does the research method do what it says it will do every time?"

If you are conducting quantitative research, these questions are relatively easy to answer. For example, you might be testing a new literacy program that promises to help adults read. Your first questions are those of validity. Does it actually give positive results? Do adults really learn how to read? The second questions concern reliability. If I see positive results this time, will I see them the next time? Does the reading program work in my colleague's community college class down the road, just like it works in mine?

If your research is qualitative, the questions are a bit trickier. Because the focus of your research is the "subject" (worker or manager or office) not the "object" (a reading program), you must ask subjective questions about reliability and validity. Qualitative researchers have reshaped these questions into the following:

- **Validity**: "Does what I am seeing here match what my experience suggests I should be seeing?"
- **Reliability**: "Does what I am describing to you about this research experience 'ring true' with your own experiences and understandings?"

Rosemary Lodge (2001) constructed a chart (see figure 8.2) to link these concepts with key questions.

**Fig.** 8.2. **Evaluating Qualitative Data** (Lodge 2001)

| Evaluating Qualitative Data | | |
|---|---|---|
| *Credibility* | **Data are authentic and believable** | • Is there enough detail from enough sources?<br>• Are the sources perceived as reliable? |
| *Confirmation* | **Verifying the validity of the findings** | • Do the people being studied recognize themselves?<br>• Do they agree that your themes get at important issues? |
| *Dependability* | **External validity of the data** | • Do others familiar with the situation trust the data as accurate and informative?<br>• Do your findings resonate with other cases? |
| *Transferability* | **Generalize: to what extent and how might the data apply elsewhere?** | • Is sufficient detail present to help readers generalize to their own contexts?<br>• Can they be generalized as a theory or model?<br>• Can they be applied to other populations? |

# Using Computers to Record and Organize Data

Researchers are not always alone in their quest to analyze their data. There are a variety of computer-assisted qualitative data analysis software (CAQDAS) applications available to help researchers code, classify, and sort qualitative data. Once mastered, these applications can save time and make analysis easier. However, they have drawbacks because they rely on generalized principles and not the specific, situational knowledge that is so often at the heart of site-specific research. In other words, these programs can take some of the tedium out of the stage where you are making sense of your data (as we did in the previous chapter), but they do not perform the work of analysis—that is still *your* job.

Further, it is possible to get caught up mucking around with the statistics to the extent that you lose the big picture of your project. It can be tempting and is sometimes appropriate to quantify or measure qualitative data, especially when an audience is skeptical about qualitative research. (Sadly, this is often the case in organizational research.) However, the appearance of credibility is not the same as real credibility! Statistical data are still simply another triangulated piece of the research puzzle you are trying to put together. Statistics, charts, and graphs can lend understanding—especially as you present your findings—but they cannot do it all.

Unless you plan to make formal qualitative research a major and ongoing part of your life (and for most of Jim's graduate students this has *not* been the case), we'd suggest that the time it takes to master a CAQDAS application may be better spent further befriending your project data. And, as Patton (2002) suggests, many researchers don't take to computerized analysis simply because they need to "get physical" with their data as part of their interpretive work (p. 446). However, if you choose the computerized route for qualitative analysis (and some do), Nud*ist and Atlas.ti are popular packages. Software reviews, advice, and some shareware can be found online.

Even if you don't pursue sorting software, there is a time and place to use technology to help you with collect, work on, and present your research. Careful organization and presentation of your data makes results easy to comprehend and communicate. For the purposes of your project, if you are using the software program Microsoft Word, you already have some charting and graphing tools to create basic visuals. Spreadsheet programs like Excel are also simple to master for basic data presentation. Try them out.

**Fig. 8.3. Using Computers to Collect and Sort Data**

---

**Computer Use in Research: An Example**

The manager and a team of action researchers in a large chemical plant designed a study about safety issues. The plant had office workers who could input the data with little cost to the organization, so data collection took the form of surveys and interviews. A basic survey, widely disseminated, provided statistical data on safety knowledge and safety attitudes among workers. Qualitative data analysis software coded key themes emerging from interviews with staff, floor supervisors, and the plant's safety education team, and helped the research team to create a theme and then analyze the different responses among these groups. For instance, differing beliefs about the causes of compliance failures were suggested in the interviews.

The software also helped the research team to translate the qualitative data into statistics, visuals, and user-friendly reports, all of which were helpful for interpreting and presenting the data. By making the data quantifiable, it was easier to communicate findings to other stakeholders. One specific advantage was that it provided a variety of persuasive charts and graphs that the manager's organization valued.

---

# Conclusion

We hope that this advice is something you can use and reuse as you process and analyze your data. Honestly, the process can be time-consuming and even discouraging at times. So count us among your critical friends who are there to offer encouragement and some straightforward guidance when it feels like you've lost the trail and are wandering in circles through the forest of your data. We can't stress enough how helpful it is to join forces with critical friends and engage each other's work. Share your work, and accept the task of both seeking and providing insights for your colleagues.

And, with as much care as you can, create *your own* insights for *your* work. Perhaps you feel as if you are a relative rookie doing research. However, here is the truth about you and your research project: other people from other places have not gained your depth of knowledge about your site-based research project. What we are encouraging you to do here (again) is to take ownership of your work. Be confident that what you see and interpret is valuable. As the researcher, you are the expert on the data you have gathered.

Remember that your work is helpful both for your organization and for others working in your area of study. Thus, trust your own insights about what you have done. But hold these tentatively. As the old Zen-like proverb goes: if you hold the bird in your hand too tightly, you will kill it; if you hold it too loosely, it will fly away. Instead hold it in a cupped hand, both firmly and gently at the same time.

Finally, we emphasize the importance of being systematic in your attention to detail for data collection. Also work hard to set up regular times (even short ones) where you can reflect and consider what is happening in your work. Collect these thoughts somewhere safe. Remember that analysis is a slow and thoughtful process. Over time, small, short visits with your data will lend deeper and richer insights than panicky marathons. Schedule these visits, and leave some time and space in between for your ideas and insights to form.

I recently was reading an online journal of a man travelling, day by day, through Argentina. In his writings, he summarized one day by saying "*Poco a poco se va lejos.*" Translated this means "little by little, one goes far." I think this best sums up the experience of completing one's site-based research as well.

# NINE

# Reporting
## YOUR RESEARCH

*You should report action research in any way*
*that best communicates with stakeholders.*

**REPORTING YOUR FINDINGS** in a comprehensive and clear way may be a challenging task. In the movie Dragnet, Sergeant Joe Friday (played by Canadian actor Dan Aykroyd) often requests "Just the facts, ma'am" for his reports. But what are the facts? Specifically, for the research projects you complete, how you will make sense of what happened in the past months as you completed your research?

The answer is that there is no "Just the facts, ma'am" component required in reporting your research. In action or site-based research, your data and field notes are turned by you into the narrative story you will call research, much like a piece of pottery is turned at the potter's wheel. Research is an open story about the past, written in the present. It is not like looking in the mirror and seeing the past reflected perfectly to your eyes. There are different shapes to research, different spins—and these spins are created by storytellers like you. The story a researcher tells is always based upon judgment.

## Your Final Report: The Story of Your Research

Today's postmodern perspectives embrace the qualitative as a challenge to the empirical-analytical belief that research can be a representation of a universally understood set of correct facts. Thus, your research project will be a historical narrative that describes your sense of what you have done and how the participants understood what was done. You will shape your research into stories. These stories are not objective, although a conscientious and truthful representation remains the ultimate aim of the research. (Remember reliability and validity? If you haven't read about this yet, look in Chapter 8.)

## A Little Philosophy Lesson

Objectivity is based on the idea that some independent truth lies "out there" and can be grasped in the same way by everyone. This concept stems from the Scientific Revolution in the seventeenth century and the Western Enlightenment that followed it. This paradigm has dominated academic research ever since.

But is there really one objective truth as the end product of all this reasoning? This detached, empirical, and rational form of study is not without its critics. Specifically, the nineteenth-century European critique of objectivity is found in the work of philosophers such as Hegel and Nietzsche. These thinkers tried to understand how historical "facts" were represented by the tellers of those facts, and how the process of representation shaped the status and nature of knowledge. In other words, all knowledge is filtered through our own unique perspectives on the world.

## About Empiricism

In recent years, varying perspectives—from the standpoints of gender or race, for example—have been systematically applied as vantage points from which to better understand the concepts and theories of research. Still, regardless of what new perspectives come along as windows through which you might view the world of your research, two activities are required if you are to understand what you are seeing. These are an *empirical account*, followed by analysis. In other words, researchers are interested in (1) what happened, and (2) what this means or how you make sense of what happened. In simplest terms, as Jim likes to explain it, the first question is, "What?" The second question is, "So what?"

Empiricism is the philosophical belief that all knowledge is derived from experience. But experience means more than simply knowledge you receive from your senses (sight, touch, sound, etc.). Experience can include your inner experiences, too; for example, what thoughts and feelings occur when you hear a particular song that was meaningful to you in the past, or when you smell an aroma that reminds you of the pies Mom used to bake? In other words, we gain experience (and knowledge) both from the outside world via our senses and from the inner world of our own thoughts, feelings, and reflections. What this means for your research is that you will use both your own reflections and your own (and/or others') perceptions. Both are important to better understanding your research.

*You can use empirical data to gain insight into trends
and relationships, to help understand attitudes and behaviors,
and to help make decisions.*

Empirical knowledge comes from both inside and outside, and from both self and others. Considering each of these general centres of understanding is important to gaining a better understanding of your research (we have used the concept of triangulation in other places) because, as empiricism suggests, research knowledge consists of constructing generalizations from particular instances. These instances are the experiences, circumstances, and insights you will use in your own, specific research project.

Remember, however, that while the tradition of research is that findings are stated in generalizations, it would be wrong to say that "My research proves…" or that research deals with "truth." Instead, research—especially qualitative research—deals with *meaning*: what is someone's experience, and what does that experience mean to him? Research also points to *correlations*: generally, when an event or activity happens, another result or event takes place along with it.

Regardless of how well you do your research project, you will never be able to say that you proved something or that you have discovered the truth. Research does not deal in absolute truths and proofs.

Instead, you will make research generalizations that are more or less reliable or have greater or lesser validity. Research seeks to achieve findings that have high degrees of probability, validity, and/or reliability. If your work is solidly empirical, this means that, as a researcher, you will have applied some systematic method of collecting data. However, your system is not enough. Analysis must be applied as you work to make sense of the data you have collected. Included in analysis are accounts both of the context of your study and the perceptions that guide you, the researcher, in your interpretations. To understand any study as fully as possible, both of these factors must be considered.

Morse (1994) presents four cognitive processes integral to all qualitative studies. These are:

- **comprehending** – the attempt to search for and learn everything possible about the setting, the culture, and the study topic
- **synthesizing** – the merging of stories, experiences, or cases that describe the patterns or responses of the participants
- **theorizing** – the development and manipulation of theoretical ideas until the most fruitful are developed
- **recontextualizing** – the development of the theory that might apply to other settings

## About Objectivity

In traditional scientific research, we strive for objectivity in our analysis, but objectivity doesn't jibe well with the more fluid and qualitative nature of action or site-based research. Trying to be objective doesn't work for two reasons. First, it is impossible for you to be objective—and why would you want to be? So much of our human experience has little to do with logic and objectivity and much more to do with relationships, which are hopelessly *subjective*. For this reason, the number of qualitative research studies in the social sciences has grown.

Second, if you claim objectivity for your work, you are saying that your analysis produces TRUTH, which, by definition, should be held to under all circumstances. Thus, your empirical analysis produces, for anyone who reads your work, nothing but a privileged sense of your own knowing. The truth—the One Great Truth, as it is defined in traditional objective research—disrespects and undermines another's interpretation, understanding, or perspective of a situation.

Believing that there can be no *one* truth leaves researchers to create meanings for their work out of the variety of possible, and generally legitimate, interpretations of what could have been seen or studied. Your interpretations become your "story" of the research you have completed. As a researcher, you have little choice but to share the knowledge you gain from your research project in the form of narrative representations, or stories. By doing so, you accept that your research is a story authored by you—a person who holds deep interests in the research she is authoring.

Thus the current emphasis of research is now less on research as a process of objective discovery and reporting, and more on the inevitably personal nature of research constructed as your story of what happened. By writing research, you engage in the activity of an author and create a text based upon the most sensible meanings you can garner from the evidence you've gathered. This process is complex, personal, and based upon your making sensible choices.

**Fig. 9.1. Research reporting styles.**

| Traditional Research Reporting | Action Research Reporting |
|---|---|
| • objective—works towards scientific truth<br>• attempts to erase researcher bias from research<br>• dispassionate, third-person writing style<br>• feelings and nuances are a bias and should not enter the reporting process<br>• trusted when methods provide factual proof | • subjective—provides multiple perspectives<br>• accepts researcher bias as part of the research<br>• often first-person narrative writing style (personal report style)<br>• feelings and nuances help the reader to understand, relate to, and appreciate the issue under study<br>• trusted when it speaks to "shared reality" |

Your research project will be constructed through your self-conscious act of writing it. Research is primarily a story about what has happened; it is not an exact factual representation of what has happened. Data themselves do not provide meaning. The challenge for you, as the author of research, is to understand the conditions under which your knowledge is created. You must ask yourself whether the knowledge you create is a realistic story of what happened. This act is not objective, but it is fundamentally moral. You must face both the complex question of how you know what has happened and the moral question of what you, as a human, are going to do with what you have come to know. That is the sense of ethical research citizenship—it is both about doing and about knowing. So as you do your final work, consider these four questions.

1. What pre-assumptions do you bring to your work?
2. How do these assumptions shape the way you construct your narratives?
3. What will you do with what you have come to know?
4. How will you represent the answers to the three previous questions to the public?

These are the questions that will shape your project. This puts you in line with others whose ultimate goal is to identify and promote ways in which individuals at the cutting edge of their professions can carry out work that is ethical and socially responsible—such as in the Good Work Project, co-directed by Mihaly Csikszentmihalyi of Claremont Graduate University, William Damon of Stanford University, and Howard Gardner of Harvard University. Good work.

**Fig. 9.2. Sharing Your Research Results**

Beyond the formal report, there are a number of different ways to share your research results to help others learn and facilitate their own professional development. Ways of sharing your findings may include:

- company newsletters and trade or industry magazines
- presentations at staff meetings
- conversations with colleagues
- creating and maintaining websites
- your actual work in your professional association.

With ever-increasing numbers of people accessing the internet, there is no discounting the importance of the virtual world. For example, our Alberta Initiative for School Improvement (AISI) research website, developed at the University of Alberta's Faculty of Education in September 2000 as part of a government-funded project, had over 9,000 hits between October 2000 and April 2001!

## What is a Master of Educational Studies Research Report?

To complete the research portion of your graduate work, you will propose, conduct, and write a final research report. This chapter provides a template of the proposal you will build *before* you undertake your research. Obviously, and ultimately, the sections outlined will also help shape the final report.

Before we outline the sections of your proposal, let us talk about the final report. A Master of Educational Studies research report is a sustained piece of individual work. The idea of the report was created because the Faculty of Education at the University of Alberta chose to have "more" than a course-based-only M. Ed., yet saw the need for an inquiry component that differed from a traditional M. Ed. thesis. Simply put, this report is "the report of a project."

Your report has a written form because we believe that educational research—and that includes yours—should be shared widely so that it might benefit the most people. As part of your graduate degree, you will complete a final product, the research report, that is approximately twenty to twenty-five pages long. We believe that this length allows the widest and most systematic opportunities for sharing what you have discovered as you have completed your research.

Although your final report is limited to twenty to twenty-five pages, this report can describe any number of varied research project "representations." In fact, we suspect these reports will vary widely. For example, your report could include descriptions of traditional academic research, other more "arts-based" forms such as dramatic representations or videos, or descriptions of curriculum projects that you have undertaken. The written report form is standard, but research projects can be quite open-ended and should flow logically from the project undertaken by each graduate student.

A research *project* is, simply, work that you as a graduate student undertake that proposes to be a contribution to the field of education. The genesis of your project derives from your own interest as both an educator and, now, as a graduate student. Your research will be applied and, as you already have read, based on an issue or problem within your specific situation or site.

## Your Project Proposal

Prior to starting work on your site-based research project, you must complete a project proposal. This proposal will guide your research project from the moment of contemplation until you have completed your research project report. You may already have begun to take notes about how you might want to complete your project. From these initial ideas, you will shape your work into a complete proposal. For educators, a project proposal is like a unit plan—and this should be quite easy for you. To give you a sense of length, most finished proposals are approximately fifteen pages long. The only reason for them to be longer rests in the length of the literature review. If your literature review is longer, your proposal will be longer.

Your project proposal is evaluated by your faculty team during the second residency for its contribution to education, its logic, its ethics, its manageability, and the soundness of its methods. Your report will be seen as successful if it "contributes knowledge to the field of education." There is no rule that the report must be completed individually; however, if it is not individually completed, you must demonstrate the extent of your individual contribution to the total report.

The following template outlines the sections your proposal should have.

## A Proposal Template: Sections of the Proposal

Templates are useful tools for putting together your proposal because they lay out the required steps (or sections). We include a template in this chapter. However, before we do, we want to suggest the purpose and intended scope of each section of the proposal you will create.

### Section I: Purpose of the Study

*(All questions are applicable.)*

1.  **What is your study about?** Provide a general but engaging introduction. *(1–2 paragraphs)*
2.  **What generated your interest in this study?** *(1–2 paragraphs)*
3.  **What area or problem does your project address?** State the area or problem; for example: "The area my research hopes to address is…" *(1–2 sentences)*
4.  **Why is your project important?** *(1 paragraph)*
5.  **How does your project fit with other work, knowledge, or other studies in your area?** *(1 paragraph)*

#### What to Include

The purpose of the introduction is to introduce the reader to your proposed research. We believe this first section works best when it is personal and when it gives some reasons as to why you are interested in the problem you have chosen to investigate. If possible, tell a story. Why do you care about the problem? What got you interested in the first place? And what did you expect you might find? In short, describe your personal interest in your problem. The style of this section should be personal, so write in the first person.

You should also discuss the significance of your work. The impact or significance of the problem or opportunity is a justification of why your research project is important and how it hopes to address a real educational problem. In this section, describe the potential impact if the problem is not eliminated or solved. Again, write in first person, but be sure to answer the fundamental question of why others (not just you) should care about what you are investigating.

## Section II: The Research Project Question

1. **What main question does your project hope to answer?** State the question; for example, "In my study I will answer the following research question:

   **What is the research question?"**
   *(State your research question in bold underneath—not in paragraph form.)*

2. **What smaller questions will you address in order to answer your main question?** State: "To answer my main research question, I must address the following questions:

   1. _____
   2. _____
   3. _____ "

   *(State these smaller questions underneath, and number them.)*

### What to Include

The purpose of the research project question section is to detail the problem you will investigate and the research question(s) being addressed. State the question your research project will try to answer. Typically, both the question and the subquestions are listed in bold. Again, the style of this section should be personal, so write in the first person.

## Section III: The Research Product

*(All questions are applicable.)*

1. **What will the "product" of your research report be?** To answer this, consider questions such as: Are you creating a research paper? A video? A report to the government? A handbook for teachers? A compilation of teachers' or students' work? *(1 paragraph)*

2. **What form will this product take?** Discuss what the product will look like. Be specific. *(1 paragraph)*

3. **Why is this form better than others?** Explain the reasoning behind your choice. *(2 sentences)*

*What to Include*

The purpose of the research product section is to describe what form your final work will be created in. Before you conduct and write about your research, it helps if you have the end in mind. Describe, as best as you can, the shape of the final product.

To maximize the value of your project for others, create a vision of a concrete form your work will take upon completion. What do you want to do with what you find out? If you want to help change professional development within your district, you may decide that it is best to conduct a workshop or a series of onsite training sessions. Perhaps a manual for new teachers is called for. Perhaps a physical reorganization of the computer lab is needed. Try to anticipate whatever might happen, and take time to describe what format your final product will look like. As stated above, this format could be a software package, video, a project report, or some other document. Whatever you believe at this point will be required, describe it.

## Section IV: The Conceptual Framework

*(This question is applicable to all project reports.)*

1.  **What conceptual framework have you adopted in producing your report?** Simply stated, where are you coming from? What theoretical perspective or practical stance are you using? For example, (theoretical stance): I am a feminist, post-structuralist; (practical stance) I have been a grade one teacher for twenty-six years in a rural Alberta school. Be as explicit as you can. *(1 paragraph)*

*What to Include*

Remember that earlier in this chapter, we spoke about biases that come with the researcher. As best as you can, describe your biases—where you are coming from. The more clearly you can describe yourself as a researcher, the more clearly another person can understand your work and how it might be applied to another situation.

## Section V: The Site of Your Research

1.  **What are the characteristics of your situation?** How might these differ from other sites?
2.  **What are the characteristics of the people you will be working with?** How are these unique? *(1–2 pages)*

*What to Include*

Here, you should describe and review information that will help the reader better know the unique situation in which you are working. For example, a rural area differs from an urban area. Your project might want to focus on "at risk" children in elementary school who are, of course, different from high-achieving senior high school students. Try to provide insight into both the specifics of your organization and its culture. Any information presented here should amplify or support the description of the problem. In short, tell about the place where you will be doing your site-based research project. Switch to an impersonal or third-person style for this section.

As well, outline those people who will be project participants. Respectful of confidentiality, your proposal should describe but not identify the people who will be participants in your research project. This list and explanation should include anyone on the "doing" side of the study and anyone on the participation side of the study. Identify and discuss anyone on the project team. Without violating anyone's (or any group's) research ethics, describe your participants in as much detail as possible. Such a list of human research subjects will also be helpful to you when you fill out your research ethics form.

## Section VI: Review of the Literature

1. **What key literature do you need to cite to show how you have come to your understanding of your chosen topic?**
2. **What key literature do you need to cite to show how your work is grounded in theory and/or practice?** *(maximum 5–6 pages for both areas; the size of the review of literature may vary greatly)*

*What to Include*

Your proposal should have a review of literature. (For more on literature reviews, refer to Chapter 5.) In this review, summarize and describe similar problems or issues as outlined in the professional literature. You should also outline any insights these other researchers have made that may be relevant to your own study. Stick to professional research here, not opinions. This section should also summarize and critique the work of others who have written in the professional literature about your topic or who have studied similar problems or issues. This professional literature should consist of journals, peer-reviewed journals, books, and other acceptable sources of information. Use an impersonal or third-person style.

If, in your review of the literature, you have discovered findings that could have potential benefit for your own study, note these. Any findings that promise a potential for success in your study should be detailed here. If they indeed hold potential, make some attempt to examine them as you conduct your own study. Any ideas you find can be briefly outlined here or elsewhere in your proposal.

## Section VII: The Design of Your Project

*(Questions 1 and 4 are applicable to all project reports.)*

1. **What, exactly, are you going to do to complete your research?** Answer this like you would write a lesson plan. Create an enumerated list (1, 2, 3...) explaining the appropriate details of your project.

2. **Are you adopting a general research approach?** For example, ethnography, action research, narrative, or similar. *(1–2 sentences)*

3. **Are you adopting specific research methods?** For example, focus group interviews, document analysis, pre-test and post-test, survey, and so on. *(1–2 sentences)*

4. **Why have you chosen to do items 1, 2, or 3 above?** How does what you have chosen fit your research report approach? *(1 paragraph)*

*What to Include*

This section should outline your research methodology. As noted earlier in this book, you need to explicate your research methods and methodology in your proposal. There is a difference between a research methodology and research methods, and this difference should be noted in your proposal. Remember, a research methodology is a general metaphor for conducting a study. This may include things like questionnaires, observations, text analyses (hermeneutics), pre-test and post-test designs, focus groups, and so on.

However, simply stating your methodology is insufficient. You need to outline your methods—that is, the specific steps you will take as you conduct the study. A reader should be able to picture what you are doing when he reads your proposal. This calls for a thorough description and explanation of the explicit steps that will be used to conduct your study. As well, address any data-gathering instruments, statistical methods, and/or analysis techniques that you plan to use in the conduct of your study.

## Section VIII: Time Frame

*(Both questions are applicable to all project proposals.)*

1. **What is your basic time line?** Briefly outline the activities you will complete and your tentative completion dates. Provide a list of tasks and dates. *(1 paragraph)*

*What to Include*

This section outlines your project schedule. As part of your proposal, set a schedule for the completion of your project. Once you have outlined your methods, this step should be relatively easy. If you have done a specific list of your methods, simply go through the list and put dates beside the items, proposing when each might be completed. Remember you are working to a time frame, so make certain your list can be completed during the time you have allotted.

This list of milestones will serve two purposes. First, it will become your project schedule. Second, it will become your personal goal—the timing you will be shooting for.

## Section IX: Traditional Considerations

*(Questions 1, 3, and 4 apply to all project reports.)*

1. **What are the limits of your research project?** Describe those choices you made to make your site-based research project manageable. List by stating: "To make my research manageable, I have chosen to limit it in certain ways. The limitations of my study are ..."

2. **What are the limitations of your research?** What won't you be able to do, even if you wanted to, due to time, ability to access everyone you need to, money, or other factors? List by stating: "The findings of my research will be limited in the following ways..."

3. **What key assumptions have you made that allowed you to proceed on your research?** List by stating: "To complete my research, I have made the following assumptions..."

4. **What terms do you need to define in your research?** Define anything that your reading audience would need to be familiar with. State: "To understand my research more completely, the following terms must be defined..." Define these terms as if you were writing a glossary.

*What to Include*

Consider the limits of what you can do with your project. It is better to be humble with findings than to overreach. Attempt to describe how your work is limited in its reach. In addition, to help achieve clarity, it is good to be transparent—for example, some terms and phrases, in some situations, mean completely different things. Attempt to be clear—define any term or situation or event that another person, unfamiliar with the situation, might not understand.

## Section X: Research Ethics

1. **Complete the research ethics form necessary to begin your work.**
2. **Come to understand the concept of ethics.** Bogdan and Biklen (1992) suggest that there are two ethical considerations in any research with human subjects: (1) *informed consent*—participants must enter the study voluntarily while understanding the nature of the study, its potential dangers, and their obligations; and (2) *protection of subjects from harm*—subjects are not exposed to risks greater than the gains they might derive from their participation in the study.

*What to Include*

What ethical considerations should you address in your study or report? (Every research project should concern itself with protecting anonymity and confidentiality, providing participants freedom to leave the study, sharing important data and checking meanings, and so on.) How have you addressed these ethical considerations? If you have not, why are these considerations not applicable? (Create a list of the things you have done to address this area.)

## Section XI: Project Requirements

1. **What are your project's resource requirements?** List any resources you need to have in order to complete your project. List these in point form with a short explanation for each.
2. **What facilities or help will you need to complete the study?** List the sites where you will conduct your research and give reasons for these choices. List any special facilities or assistance you will need at those sites.
3. **Are there travel requirements?** List any place you need to visit or travel to while you are conducting your research, and briefly say why you will travel there.
4. **Do you need special equipment?** List any special things you will need to conduct your study. These might include tape recorders, wall charts, and so on. *(1 page)*

*What to Include*

As you discuss your project's requirements, essentially you are outlining what project resource requirements will form the basis of the budget for the study. It helps to carefully consider your needs, resources, and budget. What facilities or supporting contractors might you need to complete the study? Will you have to travel out of town or overnight? Do you need transcribing help or equipment? Whatever you need should be described.

## Section XII: Bibliography
*(Both questions are applicable to all project proposals.)*

1. **Is your bibliography absolutely complete and formatted perfectly according to faculty guidelines?**
2. **Does your bibliography help others see the extent of your topic and your efforts to complete the topic well?**

## Hints about Your Proposal

Because reports are individually conceived and broadly defined, the above categories may not apply to all report proposals. Typically all proposals must review (1) where the project idea comes from, (2) how the project idea fits within the educational field and the personal history of the student, and (3) why and how the project is an important contribution to the field of education.

Your proposal is just your proposal; your research project is your actual research project. This observation may seem simplistic, but it is a reminder that each thing is necessary but should not be confused with the other. The proposal is the plan. It is a midcourse function. The best proposals are clear, detailed, and efficient. These should be lean and mean, not padded. Here are our hints for preparing a good proposal and for saving yourself valuable time.

- If there is a choice between writing short and writing long, write short.
- If there is a choice between writing clearly and confoundingly, write clearly. A research proposal is closer to the work of a pipefitter than that of a philosopher.
- Don't put anything into the proposal that will not transfer into your final project. Any extra page will have to be moved around a million times. If it isn't there, you don't have to constantly move it out of the way.
- Use your energy wisely. Finish your entire proposal during the finite time frame you have. Use your colleagues as resources, and allow yourself to be used as a colleague. You have everything you need to do the job—so work systematically and with others to complete it.
- A proposal is a group of pieces—just look at the template outline for the proposal above. Finish the proposal one piece at a time. Don't look at the whole forest and get swallowed up. Chop this tree, clear this bush, move it from the path, move to the next tree or bush. It is the Canadian way.
- Use the outline as a checklist. Celebrate each success! We repeat, celebrate the little victories. When you are finished with a section, have a little party. Don't rush on to the next without taking a breath.
- Use your critical friend infrastructure. Get together with other graduate students and read and comment on each other's work—literally and figuratively. Make this a social, community activity. Help yourself by helping each other. If you know what you want to do, start by outlining the methods. If you are uncertain, begin with the review of literature.

- Don't get lost in one thing—like the literature review—to the neglect of others. Too many graduate students get caught up in "one more article" and never get to the next section. Measure your time.
- Choose a topic that sustains your interest. If you do not have the belly for your work, it will constipate your writing and thinking. Remember that it is natural that the study you choose will, at some point or another, become burdensome. Unless you are very fortunate, expect it to happen. You can eliminate many of the doldrums by choosing something that will continue to interest you, even in those dog days.

## *A Look Ahead: Writing a Final Graduate Report*

The report that you complete for the master of educational studies is unique; however, it does come from a history of graduate research. Earlier in this chapter, we outlined the specific sections for your project proposal. But your proposal is not the end; it is only the beginning of the work.

For any graduate student, building a clear and accessible research report is crucial to the conduct of any good site-based research project. A research report allows the researcher to share her discoveries with others and is an opportunity to highlight findings and summarize results. The approach to reporting can vary, but it should be comprehensive and allow outsiders to follow the research process (Gummesson 2000, p. 211). Stringer (1999) outlines a typical final research report as having five distinct sections:

- **introduction** – identifies the problem or presents the question
- **literature review** – details what is known about the problem
- **methodology** – discusses research design and data collection
- **results** – provides a summary of data analysis
- **conclusion** – identifies the practical implications of the study.

Although you are only now completing the proposal for your research project, it might be helpful to glance at your destination—where you are going with your work. When you write up your final project report, you are limited to a length of twenty to twenty-five pages. Within these pages, you will generally include these sections.

1. **Research methods.** Provide a description of the research methodologies you used during your site-based research project. You will need to justify and support your choices of research.

2. **Data-gathering tools.** Rather obviously, this includes a description of the tools you used to collect data.

3. **Study conduct.** Describe the steps completed during the conduct of your site-based research project, including all the options you considered and attempted during the study.

4. **Study findings.** Explain the findings or observations you made during your study. To prepare for this section, you may want to consider keeping a research journal of your thoughts. Remember to link your findings to evidence.

5. **Study conclusions.** State your conclusions. These should be supported by the study findings and related literature. This would be a good place to link your findings to the findings of other studies you have read.

6. **Study recommendations.** Dare to make recommendations, but base these specifically on your findings and conclusions. Be clear how any recommendations can be supported by what you found during the conduct of your site-based research study. In other words, remember the concept of grounded theory.

7. **Research implications.** This is a description of the So what? outcome of your project. Now that you have done what you have done, what does it mean? There are two areas of *So what?* First, what do you think should happen in your organization as a result of your hard work? Second, what other research do you think should be done to further extend your work? You are now in the full-bodied flux of the research conversations about your topic of interest. In this section, you will step up and take your place in that dialogue.

8. **Organization implementation.** List any recommended changes that could improve your place of work. Detail how the implementation process might happen. What are the implications of making the changes? What are the implications of not making the changes?

9. **Future research.** As you worked through your site-based research project, undoubtedly you came to see that your work was limited. Perhaps you saw that you had missed another promising possibility for further study, but

just didn't have time to pursue it. Describe how you might proceed if you were to do the study again. Describe the implications of your research for the body of knowledge you have studied.

10. **Research project lessons learned.** Review the conduct and management of your research project. Identify what you could have done better or what processes you would now change. Your aim is to take your place among academic scholars and to help future researchers avoid pitfalls in any research they might later do.

## *Wrapping Up*

We encourage you to organize your thoughts into a well-constructed research proposal. Things always change, and you can never actually see the landscape on the map. You must be part of it. If you outline your work carefully and ahead of time, you will be more confident as you proceed on your research journey. We wish you the best. We promise that you will learn much, both about your topic and about yourself.

# TEN

# *What Happens Next?*

*Real empowerment gives workers a sense of control
over their day-to-day lives in their organizations,
and a sense of ownership over both problems and solutions.*

**YOU PROBABLY DIDN'T BELIEVE YOU WOULD,** but you now have a project in your head. And, at least for the moment, you know exactly what you are going to do. You have the vision for what your project will look like and what you must do to complete it. You have finished your proposal, and you are ready to cook.

Probably things will change—that is inevitable. However, these changes will come in due course, and they are natural. We encourage you not to become frazzled when your project mutates. We also encourage you to think realistically: the research journey you have designed in your head will not be the research journey you will travel for the next few months. In fact, in all our collective experience, we've never seen a project or research paper come out exactly as it was planned. And, think about it: if it did, the researcher would not have been open to emergence and negotiation. Finally, accept that most of the changes that occur along the way end up working out for the better anyway—so think of them not as changes, but improvements!

Your project will experience growing pains, but we encourage you to trust the system. Perhaps there is something metaphorical about the fact that all this will be over in approximately a nine-month time frame and you will "deliver" your completed project. And, just like a real-life delivery, you can have all the support in the world, but the work itself is your job alone. This is *your* site-based research project—not a group project. A graduate program in our Western academic culture is a solitary pursuit. You (generally) must complete this alone. Using someone else's work is unethical.

However, using someone else's support and feedback is not. In this chapter we hope to encourage you as well as provide you with some practical ways for you to use your support systems to your best advantage.

## First Things First: Submitting Your Ethics Review

The ethics review, as we have mentioned before, serves two purposes. One is to remind graduate students that they are, under every circumstance, to protect their participants and do their work ethically. The second purpose is to protect the university from any problems that might arise from the research.

An ethics review also keeps the university in the research loop. The job of the university's research office, then, is to ensure that academic standards, common to all universities, are upheld and that process ultimately keeps everyone—including you—looking good and doing good. Your university's research office can also be an excellent resource should any questions arise. Don't hesitate to email any issues to them about the ethics form or any other ethical questions that arise over the course of your project.

Many graduate students fear completing this ethics form, but we encourage you to go after it right away. It is not as dreadful as it looks. In fact, it is a useful exercise for you. First, it is a good review about how participants should be treated, and by completing the ethics review, you will have to get your head around your study. Use your university's ethics review form. Address the sections, answer the questions, get the proper signatures, and submit it to the research office. It should only take you two hours to complete.

Most of the specific content for the form is already part of your proposal. If your university has an online version of the form, the most practical way is to have two screens up on your computer—one displaying the ethics form and the other your proposal—and cut and paste where you can. As mentioned previously, this job takes less time than you might think.

## Before You Begin Your Research

Many students are anxious to begin their research once they've formulated a plan in their project proposals. There is nothing preventing you from doing so. However, in our experience there are a couple of things you should do first. These include two basic research steps.

**1. Envision your final format.** We believe the first step of your research journey is to answer this question: What does your project look like? This begs the question: What can a project look like? Although all project reports have a written component, they may not all be primarily written reports. Because they are action research, project reports may assume all manner of different formats—the right choice for yours depends on your needs and the needs of your organization.

For example, some projects have taken the shape of books, unit plans for teachers, workshops for health care professionals, reports to constituents or police chiefs, newly designed curriculum packages to teach needed skills in a commercial industry, and brochures that will be released to clients. The need shapes the format, which is exactly how it should be. Still, there is a requirement that part of your project report be written; after all, it is a report.

There are two other reasons. First, those who read your work need to have a sense of how you conducted your research. Second, others who follow your work need to have an idea of what you did so that they may understand your work or, in some instances, use it as a blazed trail that they might follow.

Our guess is that you underestimate how important your work might be to others. The idea that others should use your work as a model for their own seems somehow farfetched. But they will. We encourage you to not be surprised that people will be interested in your work. First, some may be interested in the content (what you found). Second, some may be interested in your methods (what you did). Remember when you read the research literature? You are now stepping up to become part of that same literature tradition—your work is your entry into becoming an academic scholar. For us, this may be the most compelling reason to do your work well.

Your first decision is to decide the format of your project. What will it look like? If you did not consider this while preparing your proposal, consider it carefully now. Without such a picture, you will have a difficult time following the map of your journey. Once you have a clear picture of what your project report will look like, you will be ready to dig in to do the actual work of conducting your project.

**2. Complete your literature review.** If you were lucky and were pushed, you have completed all the sections of your literature review. However, if you are like most people, you have only one section completed. We encourage you to complete this literature review now. This does not mean that you are finished with the literature. Every once in a while (and we will mention this again later), you need to take a little vacation from your work without actually stopping working. This is a good time to take an evening to take a new look at the literature (with fresh eyes that come from experience).

Add whatever you find into the literature review when you find it. In this way your literature review always stays up-to-date. Don't fall victim to the plight of other graduate students we know who completed their entire project and then had to go back and finish their literature review. Honestly, this happens more frequently than you would think. Not only is it completely backwards, it is a pain and does not help the student do the work as well as he could have.

# Pacing Yourself

Some less formal aspects to your work exist, and we would like to touch briefly upon these. Again, we offer the caveat that we have relied upon our long collective experience in doing and teaching research and sustaining the research activity. Use the "Needs" listed below as a sort of a checklist of activities that are important considerations for any graduate student who really wants to complete the project. We are talking about you.

## *Need # 1: Staying Organized*

Students are busy people! Like your peers, you are no doubt juggling family and work responsibilities along with those responsibilities you've taken up at university. With so much going on, at times it can be difficult to stay organized and focused, particularly once you lose the structure of classes and externally imposed deadlines. Most of us are great at meeting deadlines when someone else assigns them, but not so able to meet them when no one is looking over our shoulders! Having the stomach for your research is crucial, which is why we emphasized earlier the importance of choosing an area of research that is intrinsically interesting to you—something that will sustain your interest when the going gets tough.

A number of students struggle with the loss of structure that occurs during this stage. You've got several months of wide-open space and some big things to accomplish. However, we trust that, as part of your methodology in your proposal, you outlined the steps in your research project with some specificity, including a timeline for completing these steps. That timeline will form the basis of your time management over the next several months. We recommend getting a good wall calendar on which you can clearly post your project milestones.

At the risk of banality, we also refer you to our old friends in the story *The Hare and The Tortoise*. You'll remember Aesop's conclusion that "Slow but steady wins the race." Lawyer and best-selling author John Grisham took three years to complete his first novel, *A Time to Kill*: three years of getting up at 5:00 in the morning six days a week, writing an hour or two at a time. The idea here is that small blocks of regularly scheduled time add up to big things.

*Designing research is a creative activity.*

We encourage you to break up big jobs into little pieces that you can accomplish in an hour or an afternoon. Most of our writing on this book, for example, was done in hour-long sessions. All added up. If you really want to finish your project, you need to set aside a regular time each week to revisit it. Scheduled activities can include writing or formatting your final presentation, reviewing literature, writing and reviewing your research, entering personal journal notes, making project-related phone calls, filing paperwork, creating electronic files and emails, or scheduling activities and appointments. There is a lot to do that extends past writing.

## Need # 2: Sustaining Energy

As we pointed out above, you need to stay the course. But you also need time to rest. So here is the question: How can a researcher rest and work at the same time? Over our years of research work, we have come up with some solutions that work for us.

**Multitask the little things.** You may be the sort of a person who needs to do one thing at a time, but if you get tired of that one thing, we suggest having something—perhaps something rather mindless—to do when you just need a break. You may want to make a to-do list or job jar, and write on stickies all those little things—such as alphabetizing your bibliography—that you just need to do. These tasks might not take much time, but they are to-do's that you simply have To Do.

When we need a break from the deep thinking or the routine of one kind of work, we stop what is driving us crazy. But we never quit working. We simply move to the non-thinking aspects of the job that must be done at some point. So make your list and turn to it when you are tired of other stuff!

**Add to your review of literature.** It may sound as if we are contradicting ourselves here, because we stated earlier that you should work hard to complete your review of literature. However, we hinted earlier about how to have it both ways. When you need to take a little vacation in the middle of your work, stop for an evening or weekend and go back to some of the readings you didn't get to. Or, do a simple online search for a *couple*—understand that this means only one or two—of articles that might be added to your literature review.

What is interesting about this practical tactic is that it shows you how your thinking has been changing and maturing since you began work on this project. We find that such a literature "trip" can actually revitalize you and your work.

**Help your colleagues.** We have noted earlier the great treasure that your colleagues can be. We encourage you to return the favour. Make a pact to work with one or two of them regularly. These small breaks in the action are both helpful and restful. Some of the best arrangements or partnerships we know of involve colleagues actively and systematically meeting online to work through and read each other's material. This must be a win-win arrangement, and when these partnerships work, they really work!

## Need # 3: Keeping Notes

**Keep the notes.** Somehow, in some way, you need to discover and adopt the value of keeping systematic notes about your work. We encourage you to either (1) do formal journaling, or (2) create a regular emailing system where you can put down in words what is occurring in your research work. We encourage you to email these to a friend and keep a copy for yourself. There are three reasons for adopting a note-taking strategy: (1) it aids your research; (2) it helps with your personal development as a researcher, including those formal evaluative aspects of the personal assessment that you filled out; and (3) it aids with self-care—it is a way of tracking your own ideas and thoughts, and a time of solitude and reflection that all of us need.

**Save the notes.** Somehow, in some form that works for you, figure out how to bank your reflections and notes in a way that will serve as a source of data for a later time. We strongly encourage you to think ahead and visualize how you might analyze your data, and set up a storage and retrieval system that will work for you. Don't forget to store notes safely and confidentially.

**Revel in the notes.** Before you begin to write your final project report, it would be fun to actually review your notes slowly. Sit down with a nice cup of tea or a glass of wine, and simply read through your notes. First, read them for a general sense of what they say. Second, read them for specific themes that might emerge. And third, read them for specific citations that will be helpful in your work. Have you heard of this organizational system before? If so, and this rings true, you are catching on—your notes are a source of data that will help you complete your work.

## Need # 4: Rewriting and Editing

We love to write, so much so that we seek out every opportunity to do it. However, if you are not a strong writer and/or find writing tedious, your enthusiasm for this part of your project may be akin to what you'd feel about having a root canal. We suggest that rather than procrastinating and then trying to "eat the whole thing" in the final weeks before your deadline, make writing a normal and integral part of your project work.

**Start writing now.** This may seem odd when you have not even conducted your research yet, but when you go back and look at your project proposal, you will see that there are all sorts of little areas you can add to or improve upon for your final writing. Jim always encourages the students he supervises to—immediately—shape material from their proposal into their final writing. Doing this provides a sense of accomplishment and actually gets the work done.

For now, even if it is not your nature, become a pack rat. Save everything. If you are like others, you will find it less daunting—perhaps even encouraging—to have even the roughest of drafts started well in advance.

**Outline, outline, outline.** Outlines are maps of your whole finished project. And they are far quicker and easier to play with, revise, and organize than are reams of meandering text. We suggest that you draft an outline of your work early in the game and continue to revisit and revise this outline as your project takes shape. If you get lost and no longer can remember what—or why—you are writing, go back and look at your outline. Play with it, think about it, use this tool to help you visualize the big picture.

**Break it down.** Writing is hard work. You probably already know this from earlier assignments and projects. Go until your brain gets tired—no more. Writing for a half-hour to an hour at a time is better than not writing at all. Many people never become writers because they think they *should* be able to write for hours. In our experience, marathon last-day writing sessions are less productive and less creative than what can be accomplished in short, well-paced bursts.

**Do lots of write-throughs.** When we say "write-throughs," we mean starting at the beginning and reading while at the same time adding small changes to the work. Some people seem to sweat bullets while they are writing. They sit in front of the computer screen barely able to squeeze out words at any rate at all. What stops them, we believe, is that they are trying to do all the writing tasks—organizing, outlining, making words, and final editing—all at once. A more fruitful way to write is to split up the work into its component parts and then to do only one part at a time.

Sometimes we read and write through our writing ten to fifteen times. Every time we do so we make a little change here, a little tweak there, a little addition here, and—always—a subtraction everywhere we can make one. We never worry about the final edit until the final edit arrives, and then, because we have already been through the work so often, the final edit is easy. We encourage you to do a piece at a time—not too much, just a little. And don't worry— you can always come back and fix something.

**Know when to call in the cavalry.** It almost seems pro forma for some students to hire an outside editor. We don't believe this is necessary. There are only a few times when you need to go to this extreme. Honestly, if you are a decent writer and especially if you have a colleague with whom you have a working arrangement (a reading agreement), you do not need to hire an outside editor. However, if you are not a good writer—if you are, in fact, a poor writer (and be honest; that does not make you a bad person)—then you might consider hiring an editor.

You also have your program staff to use as resources. Make use of these people! Regular consultations along the way are much better than grief and re-writes at the end of your project when you are anxious to complete your work. Editing along the way is better for your editor, too, so don't be afraid to pass along your work in "chunks." You can also make arrangements with a fellow student to exchange editing services.

**Do your APA style right the first time.** APA style is a given—some say a necessary evil—of academic work in the social sciences. Stylistic conventions form their own language and grammar, and these are necessary. They help people in the academic community speak clearly to one another about where they have been and what they have learned. Frankly, APA style isn't that bad to work with once you've mastered the basics. We strongly recommend that you learn these basics and do it right the first time. Correcting mistakes in APA is tedious, time-consuming, and frustrating—especially because graduate students sometimes tend to leave these till the last minute.

Avoid the whole mess of revising your work by consulting the style guide up front. The areas you most need to concern yourself with are (1) providing proper references in your bibliography, and (2) using in-text citations properly in the body of your work. You can buy the APA style guide if you want to, but we don't recommend it. It is too expensive and you will not use it enough to warrant it. Save the money you would spend on the APA style guide and throw a party when you have completed your work.

Rather than spend your money, try one or more of these ideas.

- **Study and copy the style of references used in reliable documents that use APA style.** The keyword here is *reliable*—make sure the work you are using is a resource that was written by someone who knew her stuff! A strong, previously completed project recommended by your supervisor is a good starting place.
- **Consult the library.** Remember that the university library has a good system for helping students complete their projects—and they charge a

pittance compared to what an editor would charge and less than the cost of the APA guide. They include stylistic advice in their deal. Don't take advantage of them (that is, do your work well), but do take advantage of them—does that make sense?

- **Consult online style guides.** Almost every university library has a condensed version of APA style basics among their support documents. These online guides are often more succinct—and easier to use—than the actual APA style guide. Find a good one that you can easily refer to quickly, bookmark it, and use it as you write.

## Need # 5: Drawing Support From Your Team

You have a team of people who are there to help you. These include a supervisor, your organization, your colleagues (if you are smart), and your family or friends. Suffice it to say, use the members of this team. And become a member of someone else's team as well. Use but don't abuse—that is the key concept. In fact, abuse or *over*use is, in our experience, rare. Most students do not utilize their supports as well as they could. Assume that these good people want to be used and to be helpful in any way they can be. In our experience, they are both useful and helpful. They have signed on to do this particular job, so don't be afraid to ask for the help they have agreed to give.

However, ask nicely. Some students become so wrapped up in their projects that they forget that other people have lives. Ask how your support people work best, and negotiate an arrangement that works for both of you. Respect the limits of that arrangement. For instance, don't expect immediate feedback. If it happens, you are fortunate—but most people are part-time supporters who must fit this work around another work schedule.

**Your supervisor.** Here are some notes about supervisors. Most of us are quite helpful. This is obvious, because most students finish on time. That little fact is quite astounding. We encourage you to take the responsibility to keep your supervisor organized and on task—it is not their fault that you care more than they do about your work. They have a simple function, and they need to do it well. However, perhaps only a few of these people are well-organized, and many are working with a number of supervisees. You would not believe how the fates conspire to have a supervisor wait for two weeks and then, on a Wednesday morning, receive three chapters at once, all which "simply must" be read by tonight. You will be able to tell a "distant" supervisor from one who has a ton of work to do. Finally, you take the initiative to keep things in order.

If worse comes to worse and things are not working out with your supervisor, change things sooner rather than later. Contact the director of your program and discuss the situation.

## If Things Go Wrong

It is wise to ask "What can go wrong?" and "How can anything that goes wrong be fixed?" Let us offer a few examples.

### *Home and Life Issues*

Sometimes life conspires to make the completion of your project difficult. We cannot even imagine what might happen in your life. Maybe there is a new job. Something extraordinary occurs that halts the process. You become ill. You move. Your marriage breaks up. These things happen to many people, and perhaps the first thing to realize is that you are not alone.

We won't say much, except that your first order of business is to tell someone connected with your program what is happening. Seek guidance from your supervisor—you need to deal with both the university and your organization. However, because your supervisor may be part-time, ask your main faculty for the regulations and assistance. The university has a vested interest in your success and has put structures in place that will help you work through issues. Ask for help.

While it is impossible to offer more specific examples, our overall advice is to let people know what is going on and to work out a solution. These things happen all the time and people do work through them.

## Research Issues

Some students come to believe that their project is just not working. Perhaps you believe you had too few survey responses. Perhaps the anticipated help (financially or time-wise) was not forthcoming. Perhaps the anticipated results simply did not surface. And perhaps you have come to believe that you simply were wrong. All these issues can be worked through, and usually with less difficulty than you might think.

Your supervisor is your academic advisor, and your first order of business is to contact and discuss what is happening with that person. Remember, in our experience, more projects need to be retooled than not; most shape-shift to some extent away from the way they were conceived in the proposal. And most of these shifts are minor. Don't panic! Just work out a solution.

If your project simply was wrong, can you still have a project? The answer is yes. Jim's mentor at the University of Texas was O. L. Davis, who for two years in a row won the most prestigious researcher award from the National Council of Social Studies. O. L. was fond of saying that some of the best research reports are those of research that did not work. Why? Because these pieces of research tell us what we should *not* do. If your research didn't work, report that it didn't work. This negative knowledge adds to the literature in positive ways. Finally, remember that your project can change. Yes, there are deadlines for completion, but even those students who do not make these deadlines generally graduate.

# Final Thoughts

Have you considered yet the magnitude of what you are doing in your project? Your work has entered into the realm of scholarship. You are working to be one of these people whose project will be soon cited as part of the "literature." Literary critic Northrup Frye wrote a short monograph titled *Creation and Recreation* (University of Toronto Press, 1980) in which he discussed the godlike human "pull" in all of us that draws us to revel in our creations. This is the real celebration of your project. You are creating something new.

When you build or create something new as a result of your research, it is yours. Unless you explicitly agree that copyright in your work will belong to someone else, it belongs to you. And even if you agree to give up copyright, you have moral rights including the right to be named as the author of your work, unless you explicitly waive those rights. So reach clear understandings or contracts, keep good records, and mark your own work clearly (e.g. copyright © Jim Parsons, 2005). Although your copyright in an original work exists whether or not you register it, you should also consider registering your copyrights (visit the Copyright Board of Canada website for more information).

Finally, we encourage you to remember that there are two projects. The first is your actual project—the one you proposed to do. Do it well and ethically. Second, you are the project. You are becoming a scholar who is creating intellectual property. Accept that with the territory comes certain responsibilities and duties. Enjoy.

Recently, at a graduation we attended, one university stood its graduates up and had them repeat a sort of medieval oath that they would uphold the responsibilities of the position they were being admitted to—a bachelor's degree. While it at once seemed a bit strange, it did point to the seriousness of the endeavour. We encourage you to do your work with celebration and seriousness.

Good luck, and welcome to the club.

# Bibliography

Advertising Federation of Australia. 2002. The AFA agency code of ethics. Retrieved
 April 17, 2005 from http://www.afa.org.au/WebStreamer?page_id=631
Alberta Teachers' Association. 2000. *Action research guide for Alberta teachers*. Edmonton:
 Alberta Teachers' Association. Retrieved May 11, 2002 from
 http://www.teachers.ab.ca/publications/manuals/ActionResearch.pdf.
Better Business Bureau. 2000. Code of ethics.
 http://www.bbbvan.org/aboutbbb/prog_services/codeethics.
Bogdan, R. C., and S. K. Biklen. 1992. *Qualitative research in education: An introduction to
 theory and methods* (2nd ed.) Boston: Allyn and Bacon.
Bryson, J., and S. Anderson. 2000. Applying large-group interaction methods in the planning
 and implementation of major change efforts. *Public Administration Review* 60 (2), 143-162.
Carson, T., and D. Sumara, eds. 1997. *Site-based research as living practice*. New York:
 Peter Lang Publishing.
Chappell, N. L. 1998. Maintaining and enhancing independence and well being in old age.
 In *National forum on health determinants of health: Adults and seniors*. Saint-Foy, QC:
 Editions MultiMondes, 94–105, 138–41.
Corsaro, W. A. 1985. *Friendship and peer culture in the early years*. New Jersey: Ablex Publishing.
Costa, A., and B. Kallick. 1995. *Assessment of the learning organization*. Alexandria, VA:
 Association for Supervision and Curriculum Development.
Covey, S. R. 1989. *The seven habits of highly effective people: Powerful lessons in personal change*.
 New York: Simon and Schuster.
Creswell, J. W. 1998. *Qualitative inquiry and research design*. Thousand Oaks, CA: Sage
 Publications.
Denzin, N. K. 1978. *The research act*. 2nd ed. New York: McGraw-Hill.
Dunnigan, P., and E. Reid. 1999. *Women in leadership: A site-based research project*.
 Edmonton: Dunnigan Reid Consulting.

Fraenkel, J., and N. Wallen. 2003. *How to design and evaluate research in education*. New York: McGraw-Hill.

Fenwick, T. J., and J. Parsons. 2002, June. *Reading literature critically*. Course handout. Master of Arts in Leadership and Training (MALT), Victoria: Royal Roads University.

Flick, Uwe. 1998. *An introduction to qualitative research*. Thousand Oaks, CA: Sage Publications.

Glanz, J. 1998. *Action research: An educational leader's guide to school improvement*. Norwood, MA: Christopher Gordon Publishers.

Glesne, C., and A. Peshkin. 1992. *Becoming qualitative researchers: An introduction*. White Plains, NY: Longman.

Gummesson, E. 2000. *Qualitative methods in management research*. Thousand Oaks, CA: Sage Publications.

HW Wilson Co. 1963. White, E. B. Autobiographical sketch. In *More Junior Authors*. New York: HW Wilson. Also available online at http://www.edupaperback.org/showauth.cfm?authid=77 (Educational Paperback Association).

Jick, T. D. 1979. Mixing qualitative and quantitative methods: Triangulation in action. *Administrative Science Quarterly*, 24 (4): 602–11.

Lodge, R. 2001. *Evaluating qualitative data*. Unpublished document.

MacIsaac, Dan. 1996. *An introduction to action research*. Retrieved April 17, 2005 from http://physicsed.buffalostate.edu/danowner/actionrsch.html.

Marsh, P., E. Rosser, and R. Harre. 1978. *The rules of disorder*. London: Routledge.

Miles, M. B., and A. M. Huberman. 1984. Drawing valid meaning from qualitative data: Toward a shared craft. *Educational Researcher* 13 (5): 20–30.

Morse, J. M. 1994. Emerging from the data: The cognitive processes of analysis in qualitative inquiry. In *Critical issues in qualitative research methods*, ed. J. M. Morse, 23–43. Thousand Oaks, CA: Sage Publications.

Moser, J., and T. A. Herdtner. 2001. Jeff's Argentina travel journal. Entry dated December 19, 2001; updated by Jeff Moser on January 20, 2002. Retrieved October 2, 2004 from http://web.ics.purdue.edu/~moserjd/argentina/en/journal/dia4.html.

Munslow, A. 2001. *What is history?* London: Institute of Historical Research. Retrieved May 6, 2002, from http://www.history.ac.uk/ihr/Focus/Whatishistory/carr1.html.

National Staff Development Council. 2000. *Tools for schools*. Oxford, OH.

Organization for Economic Development and Cooperation. 1994. *Main definitions and conventions for the measurement of research and experimental development: A summary of the Frascati Manual*, 1993. http://www1.oecd.org/dsti/sti/stat-ana/prod/e_94-84.pdf (accessed February 2003).

Owen, H. 1997a. *Expanding our now: The story of open space technology*. San Francisco: Berrett-Koehler Publishers Inc.

Owen, H. 1997b. *Open space technology: A user's guide*. [San Francisco: Berrett-Koehler Publishers Inc.

Palys, T. 2003. *The Tri-Council policy statement: A chronicle*. Retrieved April 18, 2005 from http://www.sfu.ca/~palys/TriCncl.htm.

Patterson, L., C. Minnick Santa, K. Short, and K. Smith, eds. 1993. *Teachers are researchers: Reflection and action*. Newark, DE: International Reading Association.

Patton, M. 2002. *Qualitative research and evaluation methods*. Thousand Oaks, CA: Sage Publications.

Permut, D., Weiss R., producers, and T. Mankiewicz, director. 1987. *Dragnet* [Motion picture]. USA: Universal Studios.

Richardson, J. 2000, Feb/March. Teacher research leads to learning, action. *Tools For Schools*. Oxford, OH: National Staff Development Council. Retrieved April 18, 2005 from http://www.nsdc.org/library/publications/tools/tools2-oorich.cfm

Royal Roads University. 2000. Royal Roads University research ethics policy. Victoria: Royal Roads University. Retrieved April 18, 2005 from http://www.royalroads.ca/resources/ethics%20policy.jul13%202000.doc.

Sagor, R. 1992. *How to conduct collaborative action research*. Alexandria, VA: ASCD.

Schmuck, R. 1997. *Practical site-based research for change*. Arlington Heights, IL: IRI/Skylight Training and Publishing.

Spielberg, S., director, and G. Lucas, F. Marshall, and P. Watts, producers. 1989. *Indiana Jones and the Last Crusade* [Motion picture]. USA: Paramount.

Stringer, E. 1999. *Action research*. Thousand Oaks, CA: Sage Publications.

Taylor, D. 2001. Writing a literature review. Retrieved April 16, 2005 from University of Toronto Health Sciences Writing Centre, http://www.utoronto.ca/hswriting/lit-review.htm.

Tri-Council Working Group. 1997. Tri-Council policy statement: Ethical conduct for research involving humans. Retrieved from the Natural Sciences and Engineering Research Council. Retrieved April 17, 2005 from http://www.ncehr-cnerh.org/english/code_2/

Vaill, P. B. 1996. *Learning as a way of being: Strategies for survival in a world of permanent white water*. San Francisco: Jossey-Bass.

World Bank Group. 2003. PovertyNet Home. Impact evaluation: Qualitative methods. http://www.worldbank.org/poverty/impact/methods/indepth.htm (accessed June 2003).